MW01097823

let's make it

let's

DK

a mexican-american
culinary adventure

alfredo garcia
@freddsters

make it

Publisher Mike Sanders
Art & Design Director William Thomas
Editorial Director Ann Barton
Senior Editor Molly Ahuja
Assistant Director of Art & Design Rebecca Batchelor
Photographer Ismael Martinez
Food Stylist & Art Director Ivanna Mendoza
Chef Frida Salinas
Copy Editor Claire Safran
Proofreader Mira S. Park
Indexer Beverlee Day

First American Edition, 2025
Published in the United States by DK Publishing
1745 Broadway, 20th Floor, New York, NY 10019

The authorized representative in the EEA is Dorling Kindersley
Verlag GmbH. Arnulfstr. 124, 80636 Munich, Germany

Copyright © 2025 by Alfredo Garcia
DK, a Division of Penguin Random House LLC
24 25 26 27 28   10 9 8 7 6 5 4 3 2 1
001– 341960–APR2025

A catalog record for this book
is available from the Library of Congress.
ISBN 978-0-5938-4268-3

DK books are available at special discounts when purchased
in bulk for sales promotions, premiums, fund-raising, or
educational use. For details, contact SpecialSales@dk.com

Printed and bound in China

www.dk.com

This book was made with Forest
Stewardship Council™ certified
paper – one small step in DK's
commitment to a sustainable future.
Learn more at
www.dk.com/uk/information/sustainability

dedication

To everyone who saw my cooking videos
and decided to give me a follow and support
my foodie dreams. This book wouldn't be
happening if it wasn't for you. Thank you
for everything!

contents

introduction. 9

breakfast. 31

salsas & dips 49

tacos. 83

sandwiches 103

the carne asada. 117

weeknight dinners. 131

soups & salads 163

small plates & party food. . . .183

postres y bebidas 217

introduction

welcome

From a young age, I was fascinated by all things food-related and always wanted to jump in the kitchen to get cooking. I'd start my days watching *Zoom* on PBS Kids in the hopes they'd have a cooking segment, and I'd tune into Rachael Ray's *30-Minute Meals* on the Food Network every single day after school.

I always told myself I wanted to work in the food world, whether that was at a restaurant, on a food truck, or as an editor for a food magazine—I didn't know how I'd get there, but I knew it was my goal.

I started collecting cookbooks in college—the first one was a Rachael Ray cookbook, of course. And as a member of the Residence Hall Association, I would cook meals for our board meetings. I even got to cook a couple of times at one of the food trucks on campus. It wasn't until my senior year that I really started engaging in cooking as a full-time thing. At the time, my cousin was in the baseball minor leagues for the St. Louis Cardinals. He had a close friend, Jaime Garcia, who was a starting pitcher for the Cardinals. Jaime would hire a personal chef to cook for him during the hectic baseball season, and my cousin suggested he hire me to cook for him during spring training in Florida while I was on my spring break. I had zero idea what I was doing, but I had YouTube by my side to help me when it came to cooking my first-ever lobster tail. It was going so well that I extended my stay by a couple of days (it was worth it to miss the first couple days of classes). Immediately after graduating, I started working for him full-time.

I loved every minute of my time working for Jamie, and it was during this time that Freddsters was born. When Jaime would travel on away games, I would stay behind in Atlanta to take advantage of his beautiful kitchen and start my blog.

Why did I call it Freddsters? Even though I initially hated my cousin's nickname for me, I began to embrace it over time and realized it would be pretty memorable. I kept the Freddsters food blog going for a year, and then Jaime retired and I moved back to Chicago to find a new job. I started applying everywhere and accepted the first job I got offered, a door-to-door sales job.

I had no idea what to expect, but to my surprise, I absolutely loved working in sales. I had the freedom to work at my own pace and make as much money as I wanted to. I loved the people I was working with and I made great friends, some I still talk to today. I did sales for almost three years, but during the last six months of it, I was growing lazier and lazier because the job I loved wasn't letting me do what I was truly passionate about—cooking.

In 2019, my cousin, who knew I was growing restless at my current job, asked me to move to Texas to work for his construction company. He sweetened the deal by offering me more than I was currently making. So I packed my car and drove almost 2,000 miles to Texas. But, of course, being the foodie that I am, I added almost 200 extra miles to make a pit stop in Nashville for some hot chicken and a stop in New Orleans for beignets and a po' boy. In this new job, I was working 9 to 5 behind a desk, making the most money that I had ever made. But little did we know 2020 was going to change everything.

The pandemic came around and like everyone else, I started working from home and going crazy with all the extra time I had on my hands. So, I started cooking. I was a bit late to the TikTok game, but I decided to take my shot. I started by creating a very simple recipe—frozen yogurt made from Greek yogurt with frozen strawberries and honey blended into it. I had zero idea what I was doing, how to film, how to edit, how to do a voiceover—heck I didn't even have a tripod to hold my phone, so my cousin helped me by holding the phone for me. I posted the video and absolutely no one watched it, it got maybe 300 views within the first week.

I didn't let it get me down, I simply kept watching and learning from cooking videos on the app and would randomly post recipes with scrappily edited videos that featured horrible lighting and got minimal interactions from users. I didn't experience the overnight success that a lot of other creators did during the pandemic. It took me an entire year to even hit 10,000 followers. Sometimes it was frustrating to grow so slowly, but then I remembered my days of doing door-to-door sales and how not every person you talk to is going to give you a "yes," but the more you do something the more success you will have. So I applied that same mentality with sharing my content. Once I got my first opportunity with a major brand, Philadelphia Cream Cheese and saw how much money I could make, I immediately knew that this was my chance to make cooking my full-time job.

I started posting two videos every day, one in the morning and one in the evening, and I quickly started to see my audience grow. Some of my biggest wins early on were my Fried Egg Breakfast Taco (see page 35), which resulted in an immediate gain of over 50,000 followers over the next three days, and my Creamy Avocado Jalapeño Dip (see page 70), which was a sleeper hit until *THE* CARDI B made the dip on her TikTok AND TAGGED ME! I made Caldo de Albondigas (see page 168) for the very first time and shared the recipe—10 million views later and it's easily the recipe most people have sent me pictures of saying they loved it and that it's now a part of their dinner rotation.

Growing the loyal following that I have over almost five years of making content has provided me with so many amazing opportunities, like writing this cookbook, going to the White House for a screening of Eva Longoria's movie, *Flamin' Hot*, to DINNER WITH RACHAEL FREAKING RAY at a private dinner on a rooftop in New York, to cooking with comedian Anjelah Johnson-Reyes (I think we're best friends now). These are all things that ten years ago I never would've thought I'd have done.

I had so much fun developing the recipes in this book and sharing them with friends and family during the entire process, and I truly hope you have as much fun as I did making them in your home.

notes before you dive in!

1 I like spicy food, so the recipes in this book don't call for removing the seeds from jalapeños. However, if prefer your food on the milder side, go ahead and remove the seeds. You can also reduce the number of peppers being used in any given recipe without it impacting anything other than the heat level.

2 The cook times for all the recipes in this book are there to give you a general idea of how long it will take you to make said recipe from start to finish. That said, use your best judgement. If the recipe says to bake something for 45 minutes, but it seems ready at 40 minutes, take it out. Same goes for if it still looks under done—keep cooking it! Believe it or not, oven temps can vary widely from one model to the next. If the recipes says to sauté veggies until softened for 7 minutes, but it looks like they're soft after 4 minutes, continue onto the next step at that point.

3 I am a big believer in seasoning with your heart, it's the best way to cook. But since this is a published cookbook, I'll still gave you exact measurements for all recipes. If a recipe calls for 1 teaspoon of a seasoning you know you love, totally feel free to double up on said spice. The same goes for omitting spices you aren't a fan of.

4 Lastly, if you STILL have any questions or concerns regarding any of the recipes, slide into my DMs on Instagram (@freddsters). I promise to always try to reply.

5 Have fun cooking and share these delicious recipes with your friends and loved ones. Let's make it!

the freddster's kitchen

Just being honest—as an avid cookbook lover and collector, I get very frustrated by the long lists of "necessary" ingredients and equipment at the beginning of most cookbooks. I don't want you to feel forced to get all these ingredients or make you feel like you absolutely need them on hand at all times to make the recipes in this book.

That being said, the ingredients in the following lists are ingredients I do tend to keep in my pantry and fridge constantly. Having them in your kitchen will provide you with great results in your cooking, but if you don't have them or can't get them, it won't be the end of the world, and you can easily substitute as needed.

Cheese & Dairy

Chihuahua
Cotija
Mexican crema
Muenster
Oaxaca
Queso fresco
Queso panela
Whole milk

Fresh Produce

Avocados
Calabacitas
Cilantro
Jalapeño peppers
Serrano peppers
Poblano peppers
Tomatillos
Roma tomatoes
Red onions
Limes
White onions

Dried Spices

Diamond Crystal kosher
  salt
Whole black peppercorns
Garlic powder
Onion powder
Paprika
Guajillo chile powder
Chicken bouillon
Tomato chicken bouillon
Lemon pepper
Bay leaves
Mexican oregano
Ground cumin

Dried Chiles

Guajillo
Ancho
Chile de árbol

Pantry Staples

Chipotle peppers in adobo
Pickled jalapeños
Masa harina (white, yellow,
  blue, or red)
All-purpose flour
Dried pinto or black beans
Canned pinto or black
  beans (it's okay to use
  canned beans!)
Jasmine or basmati rice
Lard
Avocado oil
Olive oil
Canola/vegetable oil
Sweetened condensed
  milk
Evaporated milk
Dulce de leche

Fridge & Freezer Staples

Chorizo
Corn tortillas
Ground beef
Shredded rotisserie
  chicken
Hash browns/tater tots
Mayonnaise
Unsalted butter
Ice cream (because we all
  need a lil' something
  sweet at the end of the
  day)

Special Equipment

Tortilla press
Rolling pin
Comal
Electric hand mixer
Tortilla warmer
Potato masher
Zip-top plastic bags
Coffee filters
Molcajete

learn more about shopping for limes

learn more about shopping for cilantro

must-know tips & techniques

There are certain techniques and skills you'll use in the kitchen time and time again—these are my go-to's. Instead of reiterating the steps every time they're used, I've opted to include the basics here for you to refer back to as necessary.

roasting chiles poblanos

Chiles poblanos are one of my all-time favorite ingredients and if I could, I would use them in every single recipe. And as much as I love using this ingredient, I absolutely hate having to explain the process of roasting, steaming, peeling, and removing the seeds every single time I want to use it. It's a bit labor-intensive, but super easy once you get the hang of it. There are three ways you can prepare poblano peppers, as illustrated in the following steps.

method one: broil

1   Clean the poblano peppers by rinsing them under cold water and patting them dry.

2   Place the peppers on a baking tray.

3   Set the oven to broil on high.

4   Broil the peppers until they're charred on the first side, 5 to 7 minutes. Flip them over and broil on the second side for 4 to 5 minutes.

5   Turn off the oven, leave your oven door closed, and let the poblano peppers steam for at least 15 minutes.

6   Remove the peppers from the oven, carefully peel off the charred skin, remove the stems, cut a slit down the middle, and scrape out the seeds.

7   The poblano peppers are now ready to use.

method two: open flame (only works if you have a gas stove or a gas grill)

1   Clean the poblano peppers by rinsing them under cold water and patting them dry.

2   Set two of your stovetop's burners to high heat.

3   Using metal tongs, place the poblano peppers directly on your stove's grates over the flames.

4   Turning the peppers every 30 seconds or so, cook them until they are charred all over, 3 to 4 minutes.

5   Once charred, place the poblano peppers in a zip-top plastic bag, close the bag, and let the peppers steam for at least 15 minutes.

6   Remove the peppers from the plastic bag, carefully peel off the charred skin, remove the stems, cut a slit down the middle, and scrape out the seeds.

7   The poblano peppers are now ready to use.

method three: air fryer

1   Clean your poblano peppers by rinsing them under cold water and patting them dry.

2   Set the air fryer to 400°F/200°C.

3   Add the poblano peppers to the air fryer and air fry for 7 to 10 minutes on the first side or until starting to char. Flip them over and air fry for another 5 to 7 minutes or until the second side is charred.

4   Turn off the air fryer and leave the peppers in the air fryer to steam for at least 15 minutes.

5   Remove the peppers from the air fryer, carefully peel off the charred skin, remove the stems, cut a slit down the middle, and scrape off the seeds.

6   The poblano peppers are now ready to use.

For most recipes, the roasted poblanos get sliced into strips or blended, so you don't have to worry about keeping them intact. But if you are charring to use for chiles rellenos, be more gentle with them when removing the charred skins and make sure to only make one slit from top to bottom, and gently remove the seeds while still leaving the stem attached to the peppers.

The air fryer method is probably the easiest, but it will not get you perfectly charred skin on the peppers.

If charring the poblano peppers to use for Chiles Rellenos (see page 143), the best method to use would be the open flame method since it leaves the peppers with the most bite to them.

using tomatillos

Tomatillos are one of the ingredients I use the most. Heck, at this point I should find out how I can grow my own so I don't ever have to buy them again. If you've never cooked with tomatillos before, then this is one tip you certainly need to know. Tomatillos aren't green tomatoes, but they are green and look like a green tomato. Typically, when you get them at the grocery store they come in a green papery husk.

To prepare tomatillos so you can start cooking with them, you need to remove the papery husk. Once this is removed, you'll reveal the actual tomatillo. You will also notice how sticky they feel. So after removing the husks, you need to rinse them well under warm water, rubbing them all over with your hands or a clean kitchen towel until they are no longer sticky. Once you have done this you are ready to start cooking with your tomatillos.

grating garlic

One of my least favorite things to do in the kitchen is finely chopping garlic. All garlic cloves come in different sizes, some are easier to chop than others, but regardless you're going to end up with super smelly garlicky fingers. Sure, you can use "jarlic" (the finely chopped garlic that comes in those giant plastic jars), but that stuff just doesn't taste the same as fresh garlic. In comes the microplane—when I discovered microplanes, my life forever changed. At first, I would only use my microplane for zesting limes and lemons, but eventually, I also started using it to grate fresh Parmesan. Then a couple of years ago, I finally discovered the BEST use for microplanes—grating garlic. I have not physically chopped garlic with a knife or used jarlic in forever.

You don't have to worry about perfectly chopping up the garlic as finely as you need to. You don't need to worry about potentially cutting your finger off because of how tiny some garlic cloves can be. You don't need to worry about having stinky-smelling garlic fingers. You'll simply be graced with a perfect paste of garlic on the underside of the microplane that you can then throw into every recipe you'll ever cook.

And the biggest help of all is that it is a million times faster to grate four, six, or even ten garlic cloves using a microplane over having to individually chop up each one.

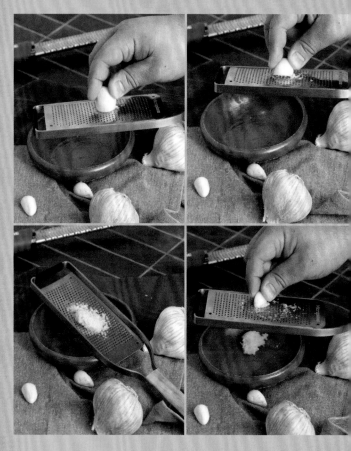

making your salsas last longer

The number one question I get asked whenever I'm sharing a new salsa recipe is, "How long will it last in the fridge?" The answer is always the same. Salsas should last between 7 to 10 days in the fridge when kept in a regular airtight container. But with a little trick I learned from my mom—adding 1 tablespoon of white distilled vinegar to the salsa right before you're ready to store it in the fridge—the lifespan of your salsa will increase to almost a full 3 weeks. The white vinegar essentially acts as a preservative to make your salsa last longer.

Lastly, not fully related, but still a good tip: if you're making any dip/sauce/dressing and are also wondering how long it'll last in your fridge, a good rule is to go based on the earliest expiration date from the ingredients used in said recipe. For example, if you're making a batch of my famous Avocado-Jalapeño Dip (see page 70), if the Mexican crema you're using has the earliest expiration date, then that is roughly how long the dip will last.

hay comida en la casa

If you're like me and grew up with Mexican parents, then you're used to the phrase, *"Hay comida en la casa,"* which translates to "there's food at home." As a kid, on basically any day after school, we'd request McDonald's or Subway as our after-school snack, and sometimes we'd get lucky—but most days we'd hear those famous words, "Hay comida en la casa." What my mom gave us usually varied, but there were three things that would always be in rotation: frijoles (beans), arroz (rice), and tortillas. With these three things, we could have a feast every single day, whether we wanted it or not.

Back then, I took these delicious foods for granted, but as I've gotten older and started living alone, I appreciate the simple things so much more. I appreciate the simplicity of some beans with fresh tortillas or a freshly cooked flour tortilla with melted butter as a snack.

If you learn how to make these three staple items, the number of recipes you can make from there for your friends and family will be endless.

In this section I will teach you the basics—from Corn or Flour Tortillas (see pages 23 and 24), Pinto Beans and how to get them refried (see page 28), and the forever favorite Red Rice (see page 25) and other favorites like White Rice with Corn (see page 26) and maybe my new favorite, Cilantro-Lime Rice (see page 26).

Use these recipes to serve alongside any of the recipes throughout this book, or serve them together for a super simple, light dinner.

the
tortillas

3 cups all-purpose flour,
   plus more for kneading
   and rolling
¼ cup lard, or any fat such
   as avocado oil, butter, or
   bacon fat
1 teaspoon kosher salt

special equipment
Rolling pin
Comal or cast-iron skillet

flour tortillas

makes: **16 to 24 tortillas, depending on size**
prep time: **45 minutes**
cook time: **15 minutes**
total time: **1 hour**

The greatest tortilla of all time. Okay, maybe I'm being a bit dramatic here, but there is simply something about a freshly made warm tortilla right off the comal that just hits different. Use these for any type of taco you want, but my preference is to use flour tortillas for breakfast tacos.

Your first flour tortilla won't be the best, it always happens—it happens to me and it happens to my mom, so the first one is always a test to see if the heat of your comal needs to be adjusted.

You have options here. You do not have to cook all the raw rolled-out flour tortillas at once. Using coffee filters, you can separate the rolled-out raw flour tortillas and refrigerate them well-covered in foil or plastic wrap. The raw uncooked tortillas will be good in the fridge for 5 to 7 days.

Leftover cooked flour tortillas can be stored in an airtight container or zip-top plastic bag in the fridge for 2 to 3 days and briefly warmed up on the comal again before serving.

make it into... *green spinach tortillas. Blend 2 cups of spinach with 2 cups of water, then add to a small saucepan and bring to a boil before proceeding with the recipe as written.*

1   To a large mixing bowl, add the flour, the fat of your choosing, and the kosher salt.

2   Add the first ¾ cup of boiling water—it has to be boiling water (I don't make the rules, my mom says it's how you do it). Using your hands, slowly start incorporating the flour and fat with the water.

3   Slowly work the mixture until it fully comes together and no dry flour remains in the bowl. This could take anywhere from 5 to 8 minutes. If your dough seems too dry, add more water, one tablespoon at a time, until it comes together.

4   Transfer the dough to a lightly floured counter. Knead the dough for about 5 minutes or until it's smooth and no longer sticky.

5   Cover the dough with a clean, damp kitchen towel and let rest for 15 minutes.

6   Once the dough has rested, divide into golf ball–sized balls. Arrange them in a single layer on your counter.

7   Begin the rolling process with the first dough ball you portioned out since it's had the most time to rest. Make sure your work area is clean, and have some extra flour nearby to lightly dust the counter and rolling pin as needed.

8   Start by flattening out the first dough ball with your palm. Starting from the center, begin rolling out your tortilla as thinly as possible using a rolling pin. It's totally okay if the first couple of them aren't perfectly round, practice makes perfect.

9   Continue rolling out all tortillas.

10 To cook the flour tortillas, set your comal to medium heat. Once hot, carefully lay out the first tortilla on the comal. Cook for about 30 to 45 seconds or until bubbles start to form all over, flip and cook another 30 to 45 seconds or until the tortilla has fully puffed up.

11 Once cooked, store them in a tortilla warmer until ready to use. Continue with the rest of the tortillas.

**learn more about
pressing flour tortillas**

1 batch uncooked Flour
   Tortillas (see page 23)
Spreadable margarine or
   salted butter
Flaky salt

Avocados, for serving
   (optional)
Black pepper (optional)
special equipment
Comal or cast-iron skillet

2 cups masa harina
1 teaspoon kosher salt
2 cups warm water, plus
   more as needed

special equipment
Plastic gallon-sized
   zip-top plastic bag
Tortilla press
10- to 12-inch (25½ to
   25½ cm) comal or
   cast-iron skillet

snacking tortillas

makes: **as many as you want**
prep tme: **none**
cook time: **about 5 minutes, depending on how many you make**
total time: **5 minutes**

Every time my mom or abuelita would make flour
tortillas, you'd find me right next to them waiting for
the freshly made flour tortillas to come off the
comal so I could snack on them. We would take the
fresh tortillas, add avocado or butter (or both), roll
them up, and enjoy. They're legit so good freshly
made you can easily have five of them and not even
feel it.

1   Set your comal over medium-high heat.

2   Once hot, start cooking the flour tortillas. Place one
    tortilla on your comal and cook for about 30 to 45
    seconds on the first side. Once it starts bubbling up,
    kind of like a pancake, flip it over and cook it for
    another 30 to 45 seconds. Flip it over one final time and
    cook for another 15 seconds or so, until you no longer
    see any raw bits.

3   Immediately after you remove the tortilla from the
    comal, place it onto a plate, get 1 tablespoon of butter
    (growing up we used the margarine from the brown
    tub), slather it all over the tortilla, and sprinkle it with a
    bit of flaky salt. Roll up the tortilla and enjoy
    immediately. If you don't want to do this with butter,
    you can mash up about a ¼ of an avocado and spread it
    around the tortilla, season the avocado with flaky salt
    and black pepper, roll it up, and enjoy. You can also do
    a combination of both butter and avocado and season
    with salt and pepper.

4   Continue this process with as many tortillas as you'd
    like.

**learn more about pressing
corn tortillas**

**learn more about store-bought
corn tortillas**

corn tortillas

makes: **about 24 tortillas, depending on size**
prep time: **15 minutes**
cook time: **15 minutes**
total time: **30 minutes**

The tortilla that goes with literally everything. Use it
for tacos, chilaquiles, tortilla chips—you name it, it
can do it.

1   To a large mixing bowl, add the masa harina and the
    kosher salt. Mix to combine.

2   Start adding the water little by little and mixing by hand.
    Start with 1½ cups of water. If you're mixing the dough
    and it looks too dry then keep adding more water as
    needed, about a tablespoon at a time. The dough is
    ready when you can form a little ball and slightly flatten
    it out between your palms and no cracks show. If you
    start flattening it and cracks are showing all around the
    edges, add more water 1 tablespoon at a time until the
    dough is ready.

3   Set your comal over medium-high heat.

4   Using a tortilla press and a cut-up plastic bag (see notes),
    grab about 2 tablespoons worth of dough, form into a
    ball, place it between the baggy, and close the tortilla
    press to flatten the tortilla. If it seems too thick when
    you open it, flip over the tortilla and press it once more.

5   Carefully remove the tortilla from the baggy and
    immediately place it on your comal. Cook the tortilla for
    30 to 40 seconds on the first side, flip it over, and cook
    for another 30 to 40 seconds. Flip it over one more time
    and lightly put pressure around the surface so that the
    tortilla starts to puff up. I usually use a clean kitchen
    towel to gently tap the already partially cooked side to
    help puff it, if needed. In total, the tortillas will cook
    between 1 minutes and 30 seconds to 2 minutes.
    Continue the process of forming and cooking the
    tortillas until you've used up all your masa. The amount
    of tortillas you get will ultimately depend on how small/
    big you make each one.

6   Once cooked, keep the tortillas wrapped between
    kitchen towels or in a tortilla warmer with a lid.

7   Serve warm with your favorite dishes.

*To cut up the plastic bag, cut down each side from where
the baggy opens. Use scissors for this, you should be able
to open and close it like a book.*

*The cooked tortillas will keep in the fridge in a plastic bag
for 4 to 5 days or in the freezer for 2 to 3 weeks.*

the rice recipes

4 Roma tomatoes
4 garlic cloves
¼ large white onion
¼ cup tomato paste
2 cups chicken broth
2 tablespoons tomato chicken bouillon
2 tablespoons avocado oil

2 cups jasmine, basmati, or long-grain rice
1 bell pepper, diced
Juice of 1 lime
1 jalapeño, with slits cut into it (see note)

special equipment
Blender

red rice

serves: **4 to 6**
prep time: **5 minutes**
cook time: **45 minutes**
total time: **50 minutes**

This rice is a great accompaniment to every dish. Serve it at parties and carnes asadas, add it to your soups, or enjoy a big ol' bowl of it straight up because it's just that good.

1 Add the tomatoes, garlic cloves, onion, tomato paste, and chicken broth to a blender and blend until smooth. You want to make sure this broth makes 4 cups of liquid.

2 Set a large sauté pan with a lid over medium heat and add the avocado oil.

3 Once the oil is hot, add in the rice and mix. Fry the rice for 6 to 8 minutes or until the rice starts getting a golden color to it.

4 Add in the bell pepper and the blended broth and mix to combine. Let it come to a boil.

5 Once boiling, add in the jalapeño, squeeze in the juice of the lime, give the rice one final mix, cover with a lid, reduce heat to low, and cook for 15 minutes.

6 Turn off the heat and let steam for 15 more minutes with the lid on. Resist the urge to lift the lid!

7 After 15 minutes, remove the lid, fluff up the rice, and serve as a side with your favorite dishes.

The addition of the jalapeño does not make the rice spicy, it simply lets the jalapeño cook in the pot with the rice. For those who do want a little spice with their rice, they simply cut a piece of it for their plate when serving.

1 tablespoon unsalted
  butter
2 tablespoons avocado oil
1 cup long-grain white rice
  or jasmine rice
¼ large white onion, thinly
  sliced

½ teaspoon garlic powder
2 cups chicken broth
1× 15.25 ounce (430g) can
  corn, drained

2 tablespoons avocado oil
1½ cups jasmine rice
3 garlic cloves, grated
1 teaspoon onion powder
2 teaspoons kosher salt

1 teaspoon black pepper
3 cups chicken broth
Juice of 2 limes, zest of 1
  lime
1 bunch cilantro, chopped

white rice
with corn

serves: **4**
prep time: **5 minutes**
cook time: **45 minutes**
total time: **50 minutes**

This is my go-to rice for any saucy dinner like my
mom's favorite Chipotle Chicken (see page 153). It's
so simple to make and you can honestly eat it by
itself.

1   Set a large sauté pan over medium heat and add the
    butter and oil.

2   Once the butter is melted add the rice and start stirring
    constantly for 3 to 4 minutes.

3   Add in the onion and garlic powder, stir together, and
    cook for 2 more minutes.

4   Add in the chicken broth and the corn and bring to a
    boil.

5   Once the pan is boiling, cover with a lid, reduce heat to
    low, and cook for 15 minutes.

6   After 15 minutes turn off the heat but leave the pot
    covered. Leave covered for 15 more minutes. The
    leftover steam within the covered pot will finish
    cooking the rice.

7   Remove the lid, fluff up the rice, and serve as you
    please.

cilantro-lime rice

serves: **4**
prep time: **5 minutes**
cook time: **45 minutes**
total time: **50 minutes**

I first made this recipe as a copycat of cilantro lime
rice from Chipotle but honestly this one is a million
times better than that one and actually tastes like
cilantro and limon. It's so good I will legit just eat a
bowl of this and nothing else, but obviously serve it
as a side with your favorite dishes.

1   Set a sauté pan over medium heat and add the oil.

2   Once hot, add in the rice and start frying for 5 to 6
    minutes.

3   Mix in the garlic and spices and cook for 1 to 2 more
    minutes.

4   Add the chicken broth and the juice of one lime. Mix to
    combine and let it come to a boil.

5   Once boiling, cover with a lid, reduce heat to low and
    cook for 15 minutes.

6   After 15 minutes turn off the heat and leave the pan
    covered for another 15 minutes.

7   After 15 minutes of resting, remove the lid and add in
    the rest of the lime juice and lime zest along with the
    chopped cilantro. Mix to fully combine.

8   Serve with your favorite foods.

beans

1 pound (450g) dried
beans, pinto or black or
any other type you prefer
1 head of garlic

1 large white onion, skin
removed
2 dried bay leaves
1 tablespoon kosher salt

pot of pinto or black beans

makes: **about 16 cups cooked beans**
prep time: **8 hours soaking time (up to overnight)**
cook time: **2 to 4 hours (start checking for doneness at 2 hours)**
total time: **4 hours (plus soaking time)**

We tend to eat frijoles with literally every meal. Heck, if he could, my dad would eat them for dessert too. Learn how to make a simple pot of beans and you'll have the start to hundreds of recipes from there.

This makes a lot of beans, but we go through them quickly. Once the beans have cooled down, you can divide them up into zip-top plastic baggies. I like to do this in baggies of 1 to 2 cups each. The bagged beans will keep in the freezer for up to 6 months. When ready to use, simply take them out of the freezer the day before you plan on using them.

1   The night before you want to cook your beans, add them to a large bowl along with enough water to cover them by at least 3 to 4 inches (7½ to 10 cm). Cover and let sit on your counter overnight or for at least 8 hours.

2   When you are ready to cook the beans, drain the soaked beans. They should have about doubled in size; soaking will speed up the cooking process.

3   Add the drained beans to a large pot, preferably a Dutch oven or even a clay pot if you have one.

4   Add 10 cups of water, the entire head of garlic, the entire onion, and the two bay leaves.

5   Turn on the heat to medium high and let the pot of beans come to a boil, making sure to mix around every couple of minutes.

6   Once the pot is boiling, reduce the heat to medium-low and place the lid slightly offset so that some steam can still escape. Make sure to mix the beans around every 15 minutes or so to make sure nothing is burning and sticking to the bottom of your pot.

7   Cook the beans for 1 hour. After the first hour of cooking, add in the kosher salt and mix to combine. We add in the salt later on in the cooking process to avoid having tougher beans that take longer to cook.

8   Continue cooking the beans for another hour. Once the beans have been cooking for a total of 2 hours, start checking for doneness. You can check this by grabbing a bean, placing it between two fingers, and squeezing it down; do this with about 3 to 4 beans. If most of the beans easily mash between your two fingers then the entire pot of beans is ready to go. If the beans aren't easily squeezable between your two fingers then continue cooking and checking for doneness every 15 to 20 minutes. Not all beans are created equal, some are fresher/newer than others and those will naturally cook faster. Keep an eye on the water level after the 2-hour mark. If they are looking a bit dry then add in more water as needed, ½ cup at a time.

9   Once the beans have been cooked, remove the whole garlic, onion, and bay leaves.

10 Use the cooked beans for whatever recipes you'd like.

¼ cup lard
1 jalapeño, finely chopped
½ large white onion, finely chopped
2 garlic cloves, grated
2 Roma tomatoes, chopped

1 teaspoon kosher salt
1 teaspoon black pepper
3 cups pinto beans, homemade (see page 28), or 2 cans, with some of their liquid (you can also use black beans)

1 pound (450g) bacon, chopped
8 ounces chorizo
1 large white onion, finely chopped
1 jalapeño, finely chopped
1 tablespoon tomato chicken bouillon
1 tablespoon paprika
1 teaspoon garlic powder
1 teaspoon onion powder
1 teaspoon black pepper

1 Roma tomato, chopped
2 cups pinto beans, homemade (see page 28), or 2 cans, with some of their liquid (you can also use black beans)
4 cups chicken broth
8 ounces chicharrones (pork rinds)
1 bunch cilantro, chopped
Limes, for serving

refried beans

makes: **about 3½ cups**
prep time: **10 minutes**
cook time: **30 minutes**
total time: **40 minutes**

Now that you've made a pot of beans, you HAVE to make a batch of these refried beans. Growing up my dad could legit not have any meal that wasn't dessert without refried beans. Enjoy them as a side with any of your go-to meals.

1   Set a large frying pan over medium-high heat and add the lard.

2   Once the lard has melted add in the onion and jalapeño, stir then cook for 4 to 5 minutes or until the onion has mostly softened.

3   Add in the garlic, combine well, and cook for another 2 minutes.

4   Now add in the tomatoes along with the salt and pepper. Mix around and cook for 4 to 5 minutes or until the tomatoes have started breaking down.

5   Add in the 3 cups of cooked pinto beans (or black beans if using) and let come to a simmer, about 6 to 8 minutes. Stir constantly to avoid them burning or sticking.

6   Reduce the heat to low and, using a potato masher, start mashing up the beans until you get your desired consistency—I like them to still be slightly chunky, but you can make them as smooth or as chunky as you'd like.

7   Serve the warm beans as a side with your favorite meals.

The cooked beans will keep in your fridge for 7 to 10 days and the freezer for up to 3 months.

make it into... *frijoles puercos. Cook down some chorizo in a large frying pan for 6 to 8 minutes, add in the lard and continue with the recipe as is.*

frijoles charros
aka cowboy beans

serves: **8**
prep time: **15 minutes**
cook time: **1 hour**
total time: **1 hour 15 minutes**

In my family, if you're going to any party or carne asada, chances are you'll be getting served a hot cup of these delicious soupy beans. They are the biggest crowd pleaser—we usually make a huge batch because everyone goes back for seconds. But this recipe is a smaller amount that you can easily double if needed.

1   Using a Dutch oven or large soup pot, add in the chopped bacon and set over medium-high heat. Cook, stirring frequently, until crispy, about 10 to 12 minutes. Remove the bacon from the pot and set aside for later. If your bacon has released a lot of fat, remove the excess fat but leave behind about 3 tablespoons of it.

2   To the same pot add in the chorizo, break it down into smaller pieces, and cook for about 8 minutes.

3   After 8 minutes add in the chopped onion and jalapeño, stir, and cook for 6 to 8 minutes or until the onion has softened.

4   Add in the spices, mix around well, and cook for 3 to 4 minutes.

5   Add in the tomatoes and cook for 4 to 6 minutes or until the tomatoes have started to break down.

6   Add in the pinto beans, the chicken broth, and 4 cups of water. Let it come to a boil and continue stirring occasionally to make sure nothing is sticking to the bottom. Cook for 8 to 10 more minutes.

7   Reduce heat to medium-low, add in the chicharrones and bacon, and let simmer for 10 more minutes.

8   Taste the broth and adjust any seasonings if needed.

9   Turn off the heat and stir in the chopped cilantro.

10   To serve the beans, ladle them into small bowls or cups and serve with a squeeze of fresh lime juice.

breakfast

strawberry guajillo jam................32

fried egg tacos 35

tater tot breakfast tacos 36

migas 39

chilaquiles verdes 42

chilaquiles rojos............................43

barbacoa 46

2 pounds strawberries, washed, stems removed, and quartered
3 cups granulated sugar

1 lime, zested and juiced
2 teaspoons guajillo chile powder
1 teaspoon kosher salt

strawberry guajillo jam

makes: **about 2½ cups**
prep time: **15 minutes**
cook time: **30 minutes, plus chilling time**
total time: **45 minutes**

I'm a lover of all things sweet and spicy. This jam is essentially my excuse to have candy for breakfast. That said, it isn't too sweet, there is guajillo chile powder along with lime zest and juice in there to help balance out the sugar. My favorite way to have this is on toasted sourdough slathered with almond butter and this jam with some flaky salt on top. But another very popular way to enjoy it is to add it on top of softened cream cheese and enjoy it with crackers.

1   Add all of the ingredients to a large saucepan set over medium-high heat.

2   Cook, stirring frequently, for 10 to 12 minutes. The sugar will dissolve, and the strawberries will start breaking down into smaller pieces.

3   Once everything is coming together to form a saucy jam-like consistency, turn the heat to high and let it all come to boil. Once at a boil, cook for 3 to 4 minutes, stirring frequently. Keep your eye on it to avoid overflow.

4   Immediately turn off the heat and carefully pour the jam into a heat-safe bowl.

5   Refrigerate until fully chilled, about 1 hour or up to overnight.

6   As long as the jam is stored in a closed container in the fridge, it will be good for up to 3 months.

Cooking oil spray
2 corn tortillas
2 large eggs
1 to 2 tablespoons salsa of choice
Salt and pepper, to taste

Crumbled queso fresco (optional)
Avocado slices (optional)
Refried beans (optional) (see page 29 or
    store-bought)

fried egg tacos

serves: **1**
prep time: **none**
cook time: **10 minutes**
total time: **10 minutes**

This is the easiest breakfast taco you will ever make and it's the first recipe I ever posted on TikTok to go "viral". I uploaded the video for these tacos before going to work and when I checked the app a bit later I had gained over 5,000 new followers. Over the course of that weekend, I gained close to 50,000 followers. What this proves to me is that simplicity is the key, because this recipe really just consists of a fried tortilla with an egg cracked right on top, and a spoonful of your favorite salsa. I have since made these tacos many, many times and I always use a different type of salsa, but I recommend a salsa verde (see page 50) or salsa macha for the best result.

1   To a medium frying pan set over medium heat, add the corn tortillas.

2   Spray one side of the tortillas with cooking oil just making sure to coat evenly. Flip over and spray the other side as well.

3   Cook the tortillas for 1 minute on one side and flip it over.

4   Carefully crack an egg on top of each tortilla making sure it stays on, it's fine if some of the egg whites slide off the tortilla, just make sure the egg yolk stays in the center.

5   Cover with a lid, reduce heat to medium low and cook for 4 to 5 minutes.

6   Remove the lid, top the eggs with the salsa.

7   Place 1 tablespoon of water on the outer edge of the pan trying to avoid the water from touching the tortillas, immediately cover with the lid again and cook for 2 to 3 more minutes or until the eggs are cooked to your desired doneness. The water will create steam to help set the
top part of the egg whites.

8   Turn off the heat from the pan and with a spatula transfer the tortilla eggs onto your plate.

9   Garnish with crumbled queso fresco, avocado, and refried beans, if using.

10 Season with salt and pepper to taste and enjoy.

8 slices bacon
1× 28 ounce bag frozen tater tots
Cooking oil spray
3 tablespoons unsalted butter
6 large eggs
4 slices American cheese

1 teaspoon kosher salt, plus more to taste
½ teaspoon black pepper, plus more to taste
8 flour tortillas
Avocado Jalapeño Dip, for serving (see page 70)

tater tot breakfast tacos

serves: 4
prep time: **5 minutes**
cook time: **30 minutes**
total time: **35 minutes**

These breakfast tacos have everything you could possibly want in a breakfast taco. Cheesy, fluffy scrambled eggs, extra crispy tater tots, and bacon—how could you not love them? Also, they come together so quickly. I like to use my toaster oven or air fryer for these and cook the bacon and the tots in separate trays at the same time. I use American cheese in my eggs for this recipe because I think it works the best, but you can certainly use shredded cheddar or Colby Jack cheese in its place. Don't forget to finish them off with salsa or some creamy Avocado Jalapeño Dip (see page 70) if you have it on hand.

1 Preheat your toaster oven or air fryer to 375°F (190°C).

2 Spread out the bacon on a baking sheet and spread out the tater tots on a different baking sheet.

3 Cook the bacon and tater tots for 16 to 20 minutes, or longer if you'd like them crispier. Once cooked transfer the bacon to a paper towel-lined plate to soak up excess grease.

4 While the bacon and tater tots are cooking, crack the eggs into a bowl and whisk them up to combine.

5 To a large nonstick skillet set over medium heat, add the butter.

6 Once the butter is melted, pour in the beaten eggs, season with the salt and pepper. Tear up the American cheese into smaller pieces and add it into the pan with the eggs.

7 Using a silicone spatula, cook the eggs, mixing them around in the pan constantly using a figure eight motion. The eggs should be ready within 60 to 90 seconds. Immediately take them off the heat.

8 Heat up the flour tortillas on your comal, cast-iron pan, or flat top.

9 To assemble the tacos, spoon on some of the scrambled eggs into each tortilla, top with a handful of the crispy tater tots and crumble up the bacon on top of each taco.

10 Spoon over the creamy jalapeño dip onto each taco or serve on the side.

2 tablespoons canola,
   vegetable, or avocado oil
4 to 5 corn tortillas, cut into
   1-inch (2½ cm) pieces
4 large eggs
Salt and pepper, to taste

for serving:
Salsa of choice (optional)
Crumbled queso fresco
   (optional)
Refried beans (optional)
   (see page 29 for
   homemade)
Flour tortillas (optional)

migas

serves: **2 (or 1 hungry Freddsters)**
prep time: **none**
cook time: **10 minutes**
total time: **10 minutes**

Not only are migas a go-to breakfast for me, but
sometimes I'll also make them for dinner as well!
There are many ways to make migas, but this is the
simplest preparation. From here you can go crazy
with add-ins such as chorizo or the Mexican trifecta
of onion, jalapeño and tomatoes to make them
Migas a la Mexicana. And if you're feeling a bit crazy
like I usually am, add these cooked migas to a flour
tortilla and enjoy as a taco. As my parents would
say, "Como vas a comer tortilla con tortilla" aka,
why are you going to eat tortillas with tortillas? I
simply say, because it's delicious.

1   To a large frying pan, add the oil and set it over
    medium-high heat.

2   Once hot, add in the tortilla pieces making sure to
    separate them as much as possible to avoid sticking.

3   Stirring occasionally, cook the tortilla pieces until
    golden and crispy all over, about 6 to 8 minutes.

4   If there is still lots of oil left in your pan, remove some
    of the excess oil but leave some in there.

5   Reduce the heat to low.

6   Crack eggs into a separate bowl to ensure you get no
    shells in your eggs.

7   Pour the eggs into the pan with the crispy tortillas.

8   Season with salt and pepper to taste, I usually add
    about 1 teaspoon of each.

9   Start mixing by breaking up the egg yolks with a spatula
    and combining everything together.

10 The eggs should be cooked through in 1 to 2 minutes.

11 Turn off the heat and divide the migas among the
    plates. Serve with a side of refried beans, if using.

12 Top them off with your favorite salsa and crumbled
    queso fresco.

13 Enjoy with a fork or add to tortillas to make tacos.

Love Story To...
chilaquiles

I will forever remember the first time I had chilaquiles as a kid.

I had no idea what I was in store for, but they completely changed my life.

Crispy tortilla chips, my mom's go-to salsa verde, some huevitos, and refried beans on the side. All simmered together until it reached perfection.

I don't know for sure, but I'm almost positive I had my mom make them for me three days in a row after that.

It was love at first sight (I mean love at first bite).

The endless ways of making and preparing chilaquiles is why I love them so much.

You can have them multiple days in a row but still have a completely different experience every time.

The combination of crispy tortilla chips simmered in salsa is pure magic.

Some chips get soggy and some stay crispy, so the texture changes from bite to bite.

On top of that, you can customize them to your heart's desire—add some refried beans and a fried egg with a runny yolk to become one with the salsa, and you'll never look back.

When it comes to the finishing touches, go crazy!

Mix in some shredded cheese for an ooey, gooey touch to your chilaquiles.

Drizzle them all over with Mexican crema to tone down the spice level if the salsa is too hot.

Pickled red onions will add the perfect touch of acidity and brightness to your plate.

This is a dish that can bring everyone together.

Talk about your love for them.

Talk about how you made yours different.

Have them for breakfast.

Have them for lunch.

Have them for dinner.

Have them as a midnight snack.

My go-to place for chilaquiles when I am not making them at home is El Itacate (locations in McAllen, Texas and Pharr, Texas). They're famous for their Chilaquiles Reketes. This version starts with a giant bed of refried black beans, topped with the chilaquiles, your salsa of choice (red or green), shredded chicken (I get it without the chicken), and melted cheese. The entire plate gets topped off with fried eggs done to your liking, sliced avocado, Mexican crema, and my favorite thing of all, the chicharron prensado (pork cracklings) in your salsa of choice. I usually go salsa verde for the chilaquiles and salsa roja for the chicharron. It's the greatest plate of chilaquiles ever.

for the tortilla chips:
20 to 24 corn tortillas, cut
 into squares
Oil for frying
Kosher salt

for the salsa:
2 tablespoons avocado oil
1½ pounds tomatillos,
 husked and rinsed
6 jalapeños
½ small white onion
4 garlic cloves
1 tablespoon kosher salt
1 teaspoon dried Mexican
 oregano
1 bunch cilantro

for serving:
Refried beans (see page
 29 for homemade)
Shredded Chihuahua
 cheese
Eggs, fried or scrambled
Pickled red onions
Crumbled queso fresco
Mexican crema

special equipment
Blender

chilaquiles verdes

serves **4**
prep time: **10 minutes**
cook time: **50 minutes**
total time: **1 hour**

Chilaquiles are the greatest breakfast food of all time. In fact, if you ask me what my favorite food is, 9 times out of 10 I will say chilaquiles. I could eat them for breakfast, lunch, and dinner (and sometimes I do!). I've been hooked ever since my mom made them for me when I was younger. Back then it was mainly a weekend thing but now that I'm older they're an everyday thing. There are million ways you can make them, but this to me is the OG way.

Since you only use the oil for frying the tortillas, you can drain out any tortilla crumbs and reuse the oil a couple times

If making for many people and to ensure everyone has chilaquiles that are perfectly sauced yet still crispy, I like to add about 1 cup of salsa or so to a separate frying pan on medium heat and tossing a handful of tortilla chips in and mixing until fully coated, then I immediately serve them. This way you can make each plate to order with the desired amount of salsa and tortilla chips and none will be wasted since leftover chilaquiles become a mushy mess.

1 Prepare the tortilla chips by adding about 1 inch (2½cm) of oil to a frying pan set over medium heat.

2 Check if the oil is hot enough by adding a piece of tortilla—if the oil immediately sizzles, it's ready. Once hot add a handful of the cut up corn tortillas and fry for 5 to 7 minutes until perfectly golden brown and crispy, making sure to give them a mix every minute or so to avoid the chips sticking together. Transfer the chips to a baking sheet lined with paper towels to drain and immediately season with salt. Continue frying the rest of the tortillas in batches.

3 Make the salsa by adding the oil to a large sauté pan set over medium heat.

4 Once hot, add in the tomatillos and jalapeños, stirring every minute or so until the veggies are getting charred in some parts, about 6 minutes.

5 Add in the onion and garlic and cook together while mixing for another 5 to 6 minutes or until the onion has started softening.

6 Add 1½ cups water to the pan, allow everything to simmer for about 5 minutes then turn off the heat and let it cool down.

7 Add the cooled down veggies along with all of the water to a blender along with the salt, Mexican oregano and the entire bunch of cilantro.

8 Blend until perfectly smooth and combined, about 30 seconds.

9 Pour the salsa back into the same sauté pan and leave on low heat to stay warm.

10 If serving immediately, raise the heat of the salsa to medium and add the tortilla chips to the salsa. Mix to fully coat and simmer for 1 to 2 minutes.

11 Serve up the chilaquiles over a bed of warmed up refried beans, sprinkle over some shredded cheese, top with the eggs if using and garnish with Mexican crema, queso fresco and pickled red onions.

for the tortilla chips:
20 to 24 corn tortillas, cut into squares
Oil, for frying
Kosher salt, for sprinkling

for the salsa:
2 tablespoons avocado oil
8 Roma tomatoes
8 dried guajillo chiles, stems and seeds removed
10 dried árbol chiles, stems removed
1 small white onion, roughly chopped
5 garlic cloves
1 teaspoon Mexican oregano
1 tablespoon kosher salt

for serving:
Refried Beans (see page 29 for homemade)
Shredded Chihuahua cheese
Eggs, fried or scrambled
Pickled red onions
Crumbled queso fresco
Mexican crema

special equipment
Blender

chilaquiles rojos

serves **4**
prep time: **10 minutes**
cook time: **50 minutess**
total time: **1 hour**

To be totally honest...chilaquiles verdes are my go-to (see page 42), but every now and then I crave them with salsa roja, which is slightly spicier than salsa verde. If you want the best of both worlds, make Chilaquiles Divorciados, half green and half red.

Since you only used the oil for frying the tortillas, you can strain out any tortilla crumbs and reuse the oil a couple times. Keep it in an airtight container in your fridge.

If making for many people and to ensure everyone has chilaquiles that are still perfectly sauced yet crispy, I like to add about 1 cup of salsa to a separate frying pan set over medium heat and tossing a handful of tortilla chips in and mixing until fully coated, then I immediately serve them.

1 Prepare the tortilla chips by adding about 1 inch (2½cm) of oil to a frying pan, set over medium heat.

2 Check if the oil is hot enough by adding a piece of tortilla—if the oil immediately sizzles, it's ready. Once hot, add a handful of the cut up corn tortillas and fry for 5 to 7 minutes until perfectly golden brown and crispy, making sure to give them a mix every minute or so to avoid the chips sticking together. Transfer the chips to a baking sheet lined with paper towels to drain and immediately season with salt. Continue frying the rest of the tortillas in batches.

3 Make the salsa by adding the oil to a large sauté pan set over medium heat.

4 Once hot, add in the tomatoes and cook for 6 to 8 minutes, turning occasionally until charred all over.

5 Add in the dried chiles, onion and garlic, and cook for another 5 to 6 minutes or until the onion starts to soften.

6 Carefully add all the cooked veggies and chiles to your blender container along with the oregano, salt, and 1½ cups of water. Blend until smooth and fully combined, about 30 seconds.

7 Pour the salsa back into the same sauté pan and set over low heat to keep warm.

8 If serving all immediately, raise the heat of salsa to medium and add the tortilla chips to the pan, mix to fully coat and simmer for 1 to 2 minutes.

9 Serve up the chilaquiles over a bed of warm refried beans, sprinkle over some shredded cheese, top with the eggs if using and garnish with crema, queso fresco, and pickled red onions.

5 to 6 pounds beef cheeks or chuck roast, or a combination of the two
2 tablespoons kosher salt
1 tablespoon black pepper
2 tablespoons oil
6 garlic cloves
5 dried bay leaves
1 teaspoon dried Mexican oregano
1 teaspoon ground cumin
½ large white onion, roughly chopped
3 dried ancho chiles, stems and seeds removed
5 dried guajillo chiles, stems and seeds removed
4 cups beef broth

for serving:
Salsa of choice
Corn or flour tortillas (see pages 23 and 24)
Lime wedges
Chopped white onion
Chopped fresh cilantro

barbacoa

serves: **6 to 8**
prep time: **15 minutes**
cook time: **4 hours**
total time: **4 hours and 15 minutes**

You might be wondering why this is in the breakfast chapter, because technically barbacoa can be eaten at all times of the day—but for me, it's a breakfast food. Growing up during special occasion weekends my mom would wake up early and go to our favorite carniceria to pick up a couple pounds of ready-made barbacoa for breakfast. Just like when we were kids, the barbacoa is enjoyed as is with corn (or flour) tortillas as tacos, with salsa, lime, cilantro, and onions. It was a breakfast of champs that I absolutely loved.

1 Cut up the meat into 2 to 3-inch (5 to 7½ cm) pieces. Season the meat all over with the salt and pepper

2 Add the oil to a large Dutch oven and set it over medium-high heat.

3 Once the oil is hot, in batches, start searing the beef on all sides until browned, about 4 to 5 minutes. Place the seared beef on a plate and set aside.

4 After all the beef has been seared add it back to the pot along with the garlic, bay leaves, Mexican oregano, ground cumin, chopped onions, the ancho and guajillo peppers and the 4 cups of beef broth.

5 Let the pot of beef come to a simmer, cover with a lid, reduce heat to medium-low and cook for 2 to 3 hours or until the beef is easily shreddable. Make sure to stir the beef every 10 minutes or so to make sure nothing sticks to the bottom of the pot.

6 Start checking the beef for doneness at the 2-hour mark; if easily shreddable, then the barbacoa is ready.

7 Turn off the heat, remove the beef and set it on a plate, take out and discard the bay leaves and dried peppers that are now rehydrated. Shred the beef into smaller pieces and add back to the pot with the broth.

8 Serve the barbacoa with tortillas, salsa, lime juice, chopped onion and cilantro.

The cooked barbacoa will keep in the fridge for 7 to 10 days or in the freezer for up to 3 months.

salsa & dips

salsa verde 50

pickled red onions 51

salsa roja 52

pineapple salsa verde................55

NOT spicy restaurant-style
  salsa 56

salsa verde cruda 57

kimchi pico de gallo....................60

habanero salsa................................61

salsa borracha.............................62

salsa de chicharron 65

salsa macha marinated
  goat cheese..................................66

enchilada dip..................................69

avocado jalapeño dip 70

cheese-stuffed tortilla chips 73

crispy panela 74

queso panela aguachile.............77

coconut ceviche............................78

2 tablespoons avocado oil
1 pound (453g) tomatillos, husks removed and rinsed
5 serrano peppers or 4 jalapeños
½ large white onion
4 garlic cloves

1 teaspoon dried Mexican oregano
1 teaspoon kosher salt
½ bunch cilantro

special equipment
Blender

salsa verde

makes **about 2½ cups**
prep time: **5 minutes**
cook time: **15 minutes**
total time: **20 minutes**

This is it. This is the main event at any carne asada. It's the one salsa you need to master and make sure you always have in your fridge. This is the way my mom has been making salsa verde ever since I was a kid, so naturally it's how I make it as well. Sometimes I will make a different version of salsa verde, but this is the method you simply can't go wrong with.

1 Add the oil to a large sauté pan set over medium-high heat.

2 Once the oil is hot, add in the tomatillos and the serrano peppers. Stir every minute or so and cook for 5 minutes.

3 Add the onion and garlic to the pan and mix to combine. Cook for 4 to 5 more minutes, stirring every minute or so.

4 Turn off the heat and let the pan cool for about 5 minutes.

5 Add the cooked veggies to a blender along with the oregano, salt, cilantro and ¼ cup of water. Blend to fully combine for 20 to 30 seconds.

6 If your salsa seems a bit too thick, add water 1 tablespoon at a time until you reach your desired consistency.

7 Taste the salsa, and add salt as needed. Pour the salsa into a bowl and serve with your favorite foods.

The salsa will keep as is for 7 to 10 days in a covered container in your fridge. Mix 1 tablespoon of distilled white vinegar into the salsa before storing to extend shelf life up to 3 weeks.

make it into... *an avocado salsa. Once the salsa verde is blended, add in 1 large pitted avocado or 2 small avocados, the juice of 1 lime and one extra teaspoon of salt and black pepper. Blend an extra 20 to 30 seconds.*

1 pound red onions
(typically 2 medium-sized
onions), thinly sliced
1 to 2 habanero peppers,
seeds removed and thinly
sliced
1½ cups freshly squeezed
lime juice
1 teaspoon whole
peppercorns
2 dried bay leaves
1 tablespoon kosher salt

pickled red onions

makes: **2 cups**
prep time: **35 minutes**
cook time: **none**
total time: **35 minutes**

Pickled red onions are addictive. If they're in my fridge, you better believe I'll add them to everything, and I believe you will too. I'm not a fan of sweet, pickled things, so these aren't sweet at all. Just tons of lime juice, red onions, and some habanero for a bit of spice. Super simple and you can start enjoying them within 30 minutes. They'll keep in the fridge for a while, so go ahead and double up the recipe because they're that good.

1 Add the thinly sliced red onions and habanero(s) to a large mixing bowl.

2 Top them off with the lime juice, peppercorns, bay leaves, and kosher salt. Mix until everything is well combined.

3 Stir every 5 minutes or so for 30 minutes. Slowly, the onions will start wilting down and becoming softer the longer they sit in the pickling liquid.

4 Store in a mason jar or airtight container in the fridge for up to 4 weeks.

5 Use them to top any of your favorite dishes, from chilaquiles to tacos to burgers to salads.

If your limes aren't particularly juicy, you can sub in distilled white vinegar for the lime juice.

The thinner you slice the onions the better. I use a mandoline, but a sharp knife will certainly do the trick.

2 tablespoons avocado oil
8 dried guajillo peppers,
  stems and seeds
  removed
8 dried chiles de árbol
1 pound tomatillos, husks
  removed and cleaned

1 Roma tomato
½ small white onion
4 garlic cloves
2 teaspoons kosher salt

special equipment
Blender

salsa roja

makes: **about 2½ cups**
prep time: **5 minutes**
cook time: **25 minutes**
total time: **30 minutes**

Red or green? The question everyone asks everyone when it comes to salsa. I've said it time and time again that salsa verde is my go-to, but every once in a while I go through a phase where all I want is salsa roja. To me, a salsa roja is always spicier than a salsa verde, but you can always tone down the spice level—you do you. This salsa is great with pretty much anything, but it's especially good on tacos.

1　To a large sauté pan, add the oil and set over medium heat. Once hot, add the guajillo peppers and allow them to fry for 15 seconds per side. Remove and set aside. Fry the chile de árbols for 15 to 20 seconds total, making sure not to burn. Remove and set aside.

2　To the same pan, add the tomatillos and tomato and cook, mixing around every minute or so for 6 to 8 minutes.

3　Add in the onion and garlic and cook for another 4 to 5 minutes or until the onion is just starting to soften up. Turn off the heat.

4　Add the cooked veggies to your blender along with the toasted chiles, 2 teaspoons of salt, and ½ cup of water. Blend until fully combined, about 30 seconds.

5　Pour into a bowl and serve with your favorite foods.

If you want a thicker salsa, use about ¼ cup less water. If you want a runnier salsa, use up to 1 cup more water.

To make it less spicy only use 2 to 4 chiles de árbol.

2 tablespoons avocado oil
1 pound tomatillos (about 20 small tomatillos), husks removed and rinsed
4 jalapeños, stems removed
5 dried chiles de árbol
½ large white onion, roughly chopped

5 garlic cloves
1½ cups pineapple, diced and separated
½ cup pineapple juice
1 teaspoon dried Mexican oregano
1 tablespoon kosher salt
½ small bunch fresh cilantro

pineapple salsa verde

makes: **about 2 cups**
prep time: **10 minutes**
cook time: **30 minutes**
total time: **40 minutes**

One day I was planning to make Tacos Al Pastor (see page 89) and I wanted to make a salsa that would go perfectly with them. I immediately thought about making salsa verde because it's my favorite, but then I came up with the idea of adding in pineapple to slightly sweeten it up since al pastor already has pineapple in the marinade. The salsa came out delicious and is perfect for these tacos, but also great to have in your fridge for topping whatever your heart desires.

1   Set a large sauté pan over medium-high heat and add the avocado oil.

2   Once hot, add in the tomatillos and jalapeños. Cook for 5 to 6 minutes, stirring frequently.

3   Add in the onion and garlic, stir, and cook for 2 more minutes.

4   Add in the chiles de árbol, stir, and cook for 2 more minutes.

5   Add in 1 cup of the diced pineapple, stir, and cook for 2 to 4 more minutes, then remove from heat.

6   Let the veggies cool down for about 5 minutes before adding to the blender. Add the pineapple juice, oregano, salt, and cilantro.

7   Blend until fully combined, about 20 to 30 seconds.

8   Pour the salsa into a serving bowl and mix in the remaining ½ cup of diced pineapple.

9   Serve with tacos or chips.

The salsa will keep covered in the fridge for 7 to 10 days.

Add 1 tablespoon of distilled white vinegar if you want the salsa to last up to 3 weeks.

5 Roma tomatoes, cut in half

1 small white onion, quartered

2 jalapeños, stems removed

2 garlic cloves

1 teaspoon kosher salt

1 bunch cilantro

Juice of 1 lime

special equipment
Blender or food processor

NOT spicy restaurant-style salsa

makes: **about 2 cups**
prep time: **5 minutes**
cook time: **10 minutes**
total time: **15 minutes**

This is the salsa you will get at any Tex-Mex restaurant that gives you chips and salsa the second you sit down at the table. It's not spicy, and we all eat an entire basket of tortilla chips with the salsa because it's always that addicting.

1   Set your oven to broil on high.

2   On a baking sheet, add the tomatoes cut-side down, the onion, and the jalapeños. Broil the veggies for 6 to 8 minutes or until charred all over.

3   Add the charred veggies to a food processor or blender, along with the garlic cloves, salt, cilantro, and lime juice.

4   Pulse a couple times until the salsa comes together. If needed, add up to ¼ cup water to thin the texture.

5   Pour the salsa into a bowl, taste for seasoning, and add extra salt or lime juice as needed.

6   Serve with tortilla chips.

You can use a blender to blend your salsa, but I like using a food processor for this salsa to leave it a bit on the chunkier side.

8 tomatillos, husked and
  rinsed
5 serrano peppers, stems
  removed
Juice of 3 limes
½ small white onion,
  roughly chopped
2 garlic cloves
1 teaspoon kosher salt, plus
  more to taste

½ bunch fresh cilantro
2 green onions, thinly sliced
1 avocado, pitted and diced
Tortilla chips, for serving
  (optional)

special equipment
Blender

◇◇◇◇◇◇◇◇◇◇◇◇◇◇◇◇◇◇◇◇◇◇◇◇◇◇◇◇◇◇◇◇◇◇◇◇

salsa verde cruda

makes: **about 4 cups**
prep time: **10 minutes**
cook time: **none**
total time: **10 minutes**

This is one of the easiest salsas you'll ever make because as the title mentions, it is raw—none of the veggies get cooked. Everything simply gets added to a blender and blended until combined. Finish it off with diced avocado and you have the most refreshing salsa for your next carne asada.

1   Add the tomatillos, serrano peppers, lime juice, white onion, garlic cloves, salt, and cilantro to your blender and blend until combined, about 30 seconds.

2   Pour the blended salsa into a bowl.

3   Add the sliced green onion and avocado and mix to combine. Taste the salsa and adjust the seasoning as needed.

4   Serve with chips or as a topping for your favorite dishes.

1 cup kimchi of choice, chopped
4 Roma tomatoes, chopped
2 jalapeños, finely chopped
½ large red onion, finely chopped
1 small bunch fresh cilantro, chopped
1 teaspoon kosher salt
1 teaspoon freshly ground black pepper
2 teaspoons gochugaru pepper flakes
Juice of 2 limes
Tortilla chips, for serving

kimchi pico de gallo

makes: **about 5 cups**
prep time: **about 10 minutes**
cook time: **none**
total time: **10 minutes**

Kimchi in pico? A couple of years ago I never would've thought about adding kimchi to my pico de gallo, but boy am I glad I did because it's fantastic. Kimchi is cabbage that's fermented with tons of spices and is very popular in Korean cuisine. It has recently become one of my favorite foods, so using it in a traditional Mexican recipe was a no-brainer for me when writing this book.

1 Add all ingredients to a large mixing bowl and mix to combine.

2 Taste and adjust any seasonings as needed.

3 Serve with chips.

¼ cup avocado oil
5 habanero peppers, stems
   removed
1 small white onion, roughly
   chopped
6 garlic cloves
2 Roma tomatoes,
   quartered

2 teaspoons kosher salt
Tortilla chips, for serving
   (optional)

special equipment
Blender

habanero salsa

makes: **about 2 cups**
prep time: **5 minutes**
cook time: **15 minutes**
total time: **20 minutes**

If you're a spice baby, aka you hate anything spicy and always remove the seeds from jalapeños, then this 1,000% is NOT the salsa for you. If you absolutely love spicy foods and want everything to be extra spicy and for your nose to get all runny, then this 1,000% is the salsa for you. It's much, much spicier the day of, but surprisingly the heat level slightly cools down a bit after sitting in the fridge for a day.

1 To a large skillet or frying pan set over medium-high heat, add the oil.

2 Once hot, add in the habaneros, onion, and garlic, and cook, stirring every minute or so for 5 to 6 minutes.

3 Remove the veggies from the pan and set aside.

4 To the same skillet, add in the tomatoes and cook for 2 to 3 minutes, then turn off the heat.

5 Add all the cooked veggies along with the salt to a blender and blend until smooth and fully combined, about 20 to 30 seconds. If needed, add up to a ¼ cup water to help it come together.

6 Serve with chips or on top of your favorite foods.

Use gloves to handle the habanero peppers as they are extremely hot and this prevents the peppers from burning your fingers. You may want to open some doors and windows when preparing this salsa to avoid having a cough attack!

2 tablespoons avocado oil
4 Roma tomatoes,
  quartered
5 serrano peppers or
  jalapeños, stems removed
1 large white onion, half
  roughly chopped and half
  finely diced
4 garlic cloves
5 dried chiles de árbol

1× 12 ounce (355 ml) can of
  light beer, such as Miller
  Lite or Modelo
1 tablespoon kosher salt
Juice of 1 lime
¼ cup chopped fresh
  cilantro

special equipment
Blender

salsa borracha

makes: **about 2½ cups**
prep time: **5 minutes**
cook time: **30 minutes**
total time: **35 minutes**

This salsa is the perfect casual snacking salsa for your next festive gathering. A requirement for any party or carne asada is beer, and this salsa has beer IN IT (hence the name, salsa borracha, aka drunken salsa). It's super easy to make and has the type of spice level that's addicting. Make this once and you'll be asked to make it for every carne asada moving forward.

1   To large sauté pan set over medium-high heat, add the oil.

2   Once hot, add in the tomatoes, serranos, and the roughly chopped half of white onion. Cook for 5 to 7 minutes or until the veggies begin to char.

3   Add in the garlic and chiles de árbol and cook for another 5 to 7 minutes.

4   Pour in half the can of beer and let the mixture simmer for 4 to 5 minutes.

5   Turn off the heat and let the mixture cool in the pan for about 10 minutes before blending.

6   Add the salsa mixture to your blender along with the salt and blend until combined but still kind of chunky.

7   Pour the blended salsa into a bowl and stir in the remaining half of finely diced white onion, the lime juice, the remaining beer, and the cilantro. Mix until fully combined, taste the salsa, and adjust any seasoning as needed.

8   Serve with chips or tacos and enjoy!

2 tablespoons avocado oil
4 Roma tomatoes
10 tomatillos, husks
    removed and rinsed
4 jalapeños, stems removed
½ large white onion,
    roughly chopped
5 garlic cloves
5 dried chiles de árbol

2 teaspoons kosher salt
1 teaspoon dried Mexican
    oregano
4 or 5 ounce (113 to 140g)
    bag chicharrones (pork
    rinds)
Juice of 1 lime

special equipment
Blender

salsa de chicharron

makes: **about 4 cups**
prep time: **5 minutes**
cook time: **25 minutes**
total time: **30 minutes**

Chicharron en salsa is one of my all-time favorite foods and something I will order from a restaurant every chance I get. This is my simpler take on chicharron en salsa, using bagged chicharrones or pork rinds you'd get from the chip aisle at your store rather than homemade. It's the perfect chips-and-dip kind of salsa, but you can also use it for chilaquiles or to top off your favorite tacos.

This also happens to be the very last recipe I developed for this book. I was on a weekend getaway. I was staying in a beautiful house in Big Bend National Park and immediately used the salsa to make chilaquiles the following day.

When this salsa gets cold it will thicken up because of the pork rinds, but you can simply warm it up again to loosen it up and add more water as needed.

1 To a large sauté pan set over medium-high heat, add the oil. Once hot, add in the tomatoes, tomatillos, and jalapeños. Cook, stirring every couple of minutes for 6 minutes.

2 Add in the onion, garlic, and chiles de árbol, and cook for another 4 to 5 minutes or until the onion has started to soften, and turn off the heat and let it cool for 5 minutes.

3 Add the cooked veggies to your blender along with the salt, Mexican oregano, and 2 cups of water. Blend until smooth and fully combined, about 30 seconds.

4 Pour the salsa back into the same pan, set over medium-low heat, and add in the chicharrones, crushing them with your hand as you add them in. Let simmer for 6 to 8 minutes then turn off the heat.

5 Squeeze in the lime juice, mix together, and serve with chips or on top of your favorite foods.

1 cup extra virgin olive oil, plus more as needed

¼ cup salsa macha or chili crisp

1 teaspoon dried Mexican oregano

1 teaspoon whole black peppercorns

½ teaspoon whole cumin seeds

2 whole cloves

1 teaspoon flaky salt

2 dried bay leaves

8 ounces (226g) goat cheese log, sliced into ½-inch rounds (see Note)

salsa macha marinated goat cheese

serves: **6 to 8**
prep time: **25 minutes**
cook time: **none**
total time: **25 minutes (plus marinating time)**

This marinated goat cheese is so easy to make and it will win over anyone you serve it to. It's great served simply with crackers or added to pasta dishes. You'll want to keep a batch of this in your fridge at all times.

1   To a 2-cup measuring cup, add all of the ingredients except the goat cheese. Stir them together to fully combine.

2   Add the goat cheese rounds to a large enough bowl or container to hold the cheese and the marinade. Pour the marinade over the goat cheese, making sure it's fully covered. If not fully covered, top it off with more olive oil.

3   Refrigerate the cheese for at least 1 hour before serving (but the longer it marinates the better it will get).

4   Serve with crackers.

Before slicing up the log of goat cheese, set it in your freezer for 15 to 20 minutes to help it firm up so you can easily slice it.

As long as it's coated in the olive oil marinade, the cheese will keep in the fridge for up to 1 month.

learn more about salsa macha

1 pound (16 ounces) ground
  beef
1 teaspoon kosher salt
1 teaspoon freshly ground
  black pepper
1 teaspoon onion powder
1 teaspoon garlic powder
1 tablespoon paprika
2 Roma tomatoes, diced
1 cup enchilada sauce

(homemade or canned,
  see page 147)
1× 8 ounce (226g) block
  cream cheese
8 ounce (226g) shredded
  cheddar cheese
Mexican crema, for garnish
Chopped fresh cilantro, for
  garnish
Tortilla chips, for serving

enchilada dip

serves: **8 to 10**
prep time: **5 minutes**
cook time: **40 minutes**
total time: **45 minutes**

Once you have a batch of homemade Enchilada
Sauce (see page 147) the possibilities are endless for
all the things you can make. So naturally, I had to
make an enchilada dip since I have been called by
many the King of Dips, and because who doesn't
love a good dip for dinner? Enjoy with tortilla chips
or even scoop it into tortillas for cheesy tacos.

1 Preheat the oven to 375°F (190°C).

2 Set a large sauté pan over medium heat. Add in the
   ground beef and start breaking it down into smaller
   pieces.

3 Cook the ground beef for 5 minutes, stirring
   occasionally.

4 Stir in the dried spices and cook for 4 more minutes.

5 Add in the tomatoes, stir to combine, and cook for 3 to
   4 more minutes.

6 Turn the heat down to low and add in the enchilada
   sauce, cream cheese, and half of the shredded cheese.
   Stir until the cheeses are fully melted and combined,
   then turn off the heat.

7 Pour the dip into an 8 × 8 inch (20 × 20cm) baking dish
   and top it off with the remaining of the cheese.

8 Bake for 8 to 10 minutes or until the top layer of cheese
   is fully melted and bubbly.

9 Remove the dish from the oven and let cool down
   about 10 minutes before serving.

10 Enjoy with tortilla chips.

- 1× 8 ounce (226g) block cream cheese
- 1 large or 2 small avocado(s), pitted
- ½ cup Mexican crema or sour cream
- 10 to 12 pickled jalapeños, stems removed, seeds removed for less spice
- ½ cup carrots from pickled jalapeños
- ¼ cup pickled jalapeño juice
- Juice of 1 lime
- 1 tablespoon chicken bouillon
- 1 teaspoon black pepper
- 1 teaspoon garlic powder
- ½ bunch cilantro

special equipment:
Blender or food processor

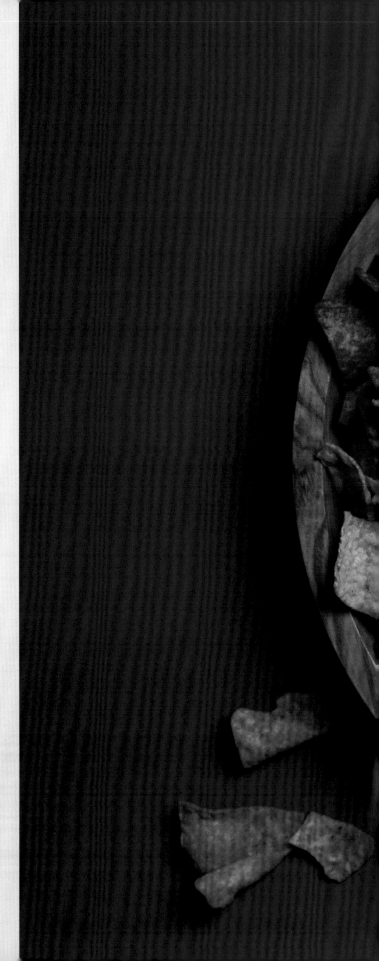

avocado jalapeño dip

makes: **about 2 cups**
prep time: **5 minutes**
cook time: **none**
total time: **5 minutes**

This is my go-to dip for parties or get-togethers. You may know it as the Cardi Dip—yes, the dip that Cardi B made a video of that went viral all over TikTok. I still can't believe that happened. It's been featured pretty much everywhere, including on *The Today Show.* It's a hit with everyone and lasts forever in the fridge because of the added pickling juice from the jalapeños. Make sure to add in some of the carrots and onions if your canned pickled jalapeños have them.

1   Add all ingredients to a food processor, container, or blender.

2   Process or blend until combined but still slightly chunky.

3   Pour into a serving bowl and enjoy with chips, or as a spread on any sandwich/burger, or topped on any tacos.

If made using a blender instead of a food processor, your dip will be a lot smoother compared to the chunkier consistency achieved by using the food processor.

20 corn tortillas (for homemade see page 24 or store-bought)
2 cups shredded Chihuahua cheese, or any other melting cheese

Avocado oil cooking spray
Kosher salt, to taste
special equipment
Air fryer

cheese-stuffed tortilla chips

makes: **40 to 80 chips (depending on size)**
prep time: **none**
cook time: **30 minutes**
total time: **30 minutes**

We all love cheese, and we all love tortilla chips, so why not combine them? Essentially, we are making quesadillas, then cutting them into triangles and air frying them until crispy. Enjoy with your favorite dips, salsas, OR use the tortilla chips as the base for your chilaquiles. Honestly don't know why I didn't make these sooner, but better late than never!

1 Set your comal or large skillet over medium-high heat.

2 Assemble the quesadillas by topping each tortilla with 1 to 2 tablespoons of shredded cheese, making sure to spread it out as evenly as possible, then place a second tortilla on top.

3 Spray the comal with oil. Place as many quesadillas as you can fit onto the comal and then spray the tops with oil.

4 Cook for 2 to 3 minutes on the first side, then flip and cook for another 2 minutes on the second side. Set aside the cooked quesadillas on a large cutting board.

5 Continue the cooking process to make the remaining quesadillas.

6 Preheat your air fryer to 400°F (200°C).

7 Cut the quesadillas into triangles (either 4 large triangles or 8 smaller triangles per quesadilla).

8 For easy cleanup, line a baking sheet with foil, place the tortilla chips onto the sheet in a single layer, and spray the tops with oil.

9 Air fry the tortilla chips until golden brown and crispy, about 7 to 10 minutes. Do this in batches if necessary.

10 Once out of the air fryer, immediately sprinkle them with salt.

11 Serve immediately with your favorite dips/salsas.

These tortilla chips are best served and enjoyed the day of. Once stored in the fridge for another day, you will need to reheat them. To reheat, place them in your air fryer at 350°F (180°C) for 5 to 7 minutes or until warmed through.

learn more about making cheese-stuffed tortilla chips

for the crispy panela:
1 pound (16 ounces) wheel
 of queso panela, cut into
 ½-inch (1cm) planks
1 cup all purpose flour
1 teaspoon kosher salt,
 plus more for sprinkling
1 teaspoon black pepper
1 teaspoon paprika
1 teaspoon garlic powder
1 teaspoon onion salt
2 eggs
½ cup whole milk
2 cups panko
 bread crumbs

Oil, for frying
1 batch Avocado Jalapeño
 Dip (see page 70)

special equipment
Blender

crispy panela
with avocado jalapeño dip

serves: **6**
prep time: **10 minutes**
cook time: **20 minutes**
total time: **30 minutes**

Appetizers are my favorite part about going out to eat at restaurants because that is often where you'll see the chef's creativity shine. This recipe is 1000% one I would put on the appetizer menu if I had a restaurant. Think of this as the Mexican answer to mozzarella sticks. Crispy panela cheese breaded and fried, served on a bed of creamy, spicy avocado dip. A sprinkling of pickled red onions adds acidity to cut through the fattiness from the cheese and avocado. Everyone will be fighting for the last piece.

1 Set up the dredging station by starting with a large bowl or baking sheet, add the flour and all the spices, mix to combine. In another bowl or baking sheet, add the eggs and milk, whisk to combine. To the third and final bowl or baking sheet, add in the panko bread crumbs.

2 Working one slice of cheese at a time, pass them through the seasoned flour, making sure to coat well all over; then pass it through the beaten eggs, making sure to coat well all over; and lastly place them into the bread crumbs, cover well, making sure to pack it in. Continue with all of the queso panela planks.

3 To a large frying pan, add enough oil to cover the bottom of the pan by at least ½ inch (1cm). Set over medium heat.

4 Once the oil is hot (test it by sprinkling in a pinch of bread crumbs to see if it sizzles), working in batches, fry up the queso panela until browned and crispy on both sides, about 2 to 3 minutes per side. Place on a paper towel-lined plate or baking sheet to soak up any excess oil. Immediately sprinkle them with salt.

5 To serve, spread some of the avocado dip on a plate, top it with a piece of fried panela and top the cheese with pickled red onions.

 learn more about queso panela

½ cup soy sauce

½ cup fresh lime juice

2 tablespoons Worcestershire sauce

1 tablespoon Jugo Maggi

1 jalapeño, stem removed

2 garlic cloves

Cooking oil spray

12 ounces (340g) queso panela, sliced into ½-inch (1.3cm) slices

¼ small red onion, thinly sliced

1 English cucumber, thinly sliced

1 avocado, pitted and thinly sliced

1 serrano pepper, stem removed and thinly sliced into rings

Fresh cilantro leaves, for garnish

Tostadas, for serving

special equipment
Blender

queso panela aguachile

serves: **4 to 6**
prep time: **5 minutes**
cook time: **10 minutes**
total time: **15 minutes**

Queso panela is one of my favorite cheeses. So much so that I always need to be stocked with it in the fridge. Pan-frying is my preferred way to enjoy this cheese—it's so firm that it doesn't melt. This aguachile is perfect for vegetarians and meat lovers alike, it feels like you're eating meat even though you're not.

1 To a blender, add in the soy sauce, lime juice, Worcestershire sauce, Jugo Maggi, jalapeño, and garlic cloves. Blend until smooth and fully combined, about 20 to 30 seconds. Set aside while you prepare the queso panela.

2 Set a large skillet over medium heat and spray with oil.

3 Once hot, add in the queso panela slices in a single layer.

4 Cook for 2 minutes, flip, and cook for another 2 minutes.

5 Remove the cheese from the pan and place on a large serving tray or plate.

6 In whatever way you like, spread out the onion, cucumber, avocado, and serranos all around the plate and on top of the queso panela.

7 Pour the sauce on top. Finish it off by garnishing with cilantro.

8 Serve with tostadas.

Jugo Maggi, if you've never had it, is something like a mix between soy sauce and Worcestershire sauce. It's very potent and a little goes a long way.

2 pounds (32 ounces) large
   shrimp, peeled, deveined,
   and tails removed
1½ cups fresh lime juice
1× 13.5 ounces (400 ml) can
   coconut milk
2 teaspoons kosher salt
2 serrano peppers, stems
   removed and thinly sliced
   into rings

1 cucumber, thinly sliced
¼ small red onion, thinly
   sliced
½ large bunch fresh
   cilantro, chopped
Flaky salt, for finishing
Tostadas or saltine crackers,
   for serving
Thinly sliced avocado, for
   serving

coconut ceviche

serves: **6 to 8**
prep time: **30 minutes**
cook time: **none**
total time: **30 minutes (plus marinating time)**

I have made many versions of this ceviche ever
since I first had it at Suerte in Austin, Texas. I first
made it for a collaboration with my friend Aaron
Alterman. Then I made a slightly different take on it
for a family dinner. And now here I am offering yet
another interpretation for you all to enjoy. The
moral of this story is that it's completely okay to
make the same "recipe" slightly different every time
you make it. Ceviche is one of those dishes that
doesn't require the use of exact measurements to
yield a great dish. That being said, I have provided
exact measurements for you here (but feel free to
adjust any ingredients to your liking).

1   Carefully butterfly the shrimp down the middle and
    open them like a book.

2   Add the shrimp to a large bowl along with 1 cup of the
    lime juice. Mix to combine and cover with plastic wrap.

3   Refrigerate the shrimp for an hour and a half.

4   Remove the shrimp from the lime juice (but reserve the
    lime juice) and arrange on a large serving plate.

5   To the bowl with the remaining lime juice, add in the
    coconut milk, the remaining ½ cup of lime juice, and
    the salt, and mix to combine.

6   Pour the coconut-lime mixture over the shrimp.

7   Spread the thinly sliced serrano, cucumber, and red
    onions over the serving plate with the shrimp.

8   Finish off the platter with flaky salt.

9   Serve with tostadas or saltine crackers and thinly sliced
    avocado.

tacos

carnitas 86

al pastor...................................89

picadillo 90

tacos de fideo seco......................93

guac egg salad tacos 94

costra de calabaza......................95

pork belly kimchi tacos 96

bulgogi tacos 99

jalapeño popper tacos.............100

Love Story To...
tacos

Tacos are THAT guy (or girl). I've had them for breakfast, lunch, dinner, and even dessert (we miss you Choco Taco). Corn or flour tortillas? I'll take them both. With a meat filling or veggie filling, I will devour them regardless.

How do you pick whether to go with a corn or flour tortilla? My philosophy behind this is, if I'm having a breakfast taco, most of the time it will be with flour tortillas. If it's a taco any other time of the day, then it's with a corn tortilla. Unless that taco is a beer-battered fish taco, then maybe I will have it on a flour tortilla. You obviously don't have to listen to me, but that's how I like to look at it. I've had many delicious breakfast tacos on corn tortillas, but flour tortillas for breakfast tacos just hit different.

There is something so satisfying about being able to stuff anything into a tortilla, top it with salsa and lime, and dig right in. I have made many, many tacos in my time, from classic tacos de asada and tacos al pastor to crazier nontraditional tacos like a jalapeño popper taco and pork belly kimchi tacos. Needless to say, not every taco will be 100% Mexican. And that's another reason why I love them so much.

Tacos don't only have to be a homemade affair—there's no better feeling than going to a taqueria and getting tacos delivered straight to your table. One of my recent go-to favorites for tacos is from Ana Liz Taqueria in Mission, Texas. Chef and Owner Ana Liz Pulido won a James Beard Award in 2024 for Best Chef Texas, and *Texas Monthly* named her tacos the best in Texas—for good reason. Her tortillas are fully made from scratch as they nixtamalize their corn and grind it in-house. The carne asada is on a whole other level, perfectly cooked through but still juicy and tender. She gives you the option to pick corn or flour tortillas, and both are great options, so just get more than two tacos so you can try them both.

An honorable mention goes to the many gas stations offering basic breakfast tacos on HUGE flour tortillas at any Stripes. Breakfast tacos at a gas station? You have to experience them at least once, and make sure it is the Q Taco. It's a South Texas special!

2 pounds (907g) lard
5 to 6 pounds (2 to 2¾ kg)
   boneless pork shoulder,
   cut into 2- to 3-inch (5
   to 6½ cm) pieces
1 cup Mexican Coke
1 orange
1 head of garlic
½ large white onion,
   halved
6 dried bay leaves

1 teaspoon whole cloves
1 teaspoon whole
   peppercorns
2 tablespoons kosher salt

for serving:
Corn or Flour Tortillas (for
   homemade see pages 23
   and 24 or store-bought)
Salsa of choice
Chopped fresh cilantro
Chopped white onion

carnitas

serves: **6 to 8**
prep time: **5 minutes**
cook time: **about 3½ hours**
total time: **3 hours 35 minutes**

When I first posted my recipe online for these carnitas, I didn't think anything of it. But they were an immediate hit and are still one of my most popular recipes to date. To me, these are mostly a breakfast item. Growing up in Chicago, my parents never made carnitas because there were so many amazing mom-and-pop shops on every corner serving up moist and juicy carnitas on the weekends. So I never knew how easy they were to make until I moved out of Chicago and made them myself. This recipe may seem intimidating, but it's really not.

Even if you stir while cooking the pork, some ingredients may still stick and burn. If this happens after you've dumped out the rest of the lard and ingredients, add about a tablespoon of dish soap, fill up halfway with water, mix to combine, and set the pot on your stove on medium-high heat to come to a boil. Once boiling, use a wooden spoon to scrape the bottom of the pot; most of the stuck burnt food should easily come off.

The cooked carnitas will keep in your fridge for 7 to 10 days or will keep in the freezer for up to 3 months.

1   Set a large Dutch oven over medium-high heat and add the lard.

2   Once the lard has melted, fry the pieces of pork in batches until golden brown all over, 4 to 6 minutes. The pork will still be raw on the inside but will finish cooking later. Once seared all over, remove the pork pieces, set them on a plate, and continue searing the rest of the pork.

3   Once all the pork has been seared, reduce the heat to medium and add all the pork back into the pot along with the Mexican Coke. Cut the orange in half, squeeze in the juice, and add both squeezed halves of the orange into the pot as well. Cut the head of garlic across the diameter to expose all the garlic cloves and add to the pot along with the white onion, bay leaves, whole cloves, and peppercorns. Mix well to combine and cook for 30 minutes.

4   To a cup add ½ cup of warm water and the salt. Stir to dissolve the salt.

5   After 30 minutes of cooking, add the salt-water mixture to the pot and stir to combine.

6   Let the pot come back to a simmer after adding the water. Reduce heat to low and continue cooking, stirring every 5 minutes or so to make sure nothing sticks/burns to the bottom of the pot.

7   Continue cooking the pork while stirring every 5 minutes or so for the next 2 to 2½ hours. You can start checking the pork for doneness after 1½ hours. The pork is ready when it's easily shreddable.

8   Once the pork is cooked and ready, turn off the heat, remove the pork from the pot, and shred it into smaller bite-size pieces.

9   Taste the pork and season with any extra salt if needed.

10 Serve the carnitas warm with tortillas, salsa, chopped cilantro, and onions.

5 to 6 pounds (2 to 2¾ kg) boneless pork shoulder

For the marinade:
2 tablespoons avocado oil
8 dried guajillo peppers, stems and seeds removed
2 dried ancho peppers, stems and seeds removed
1 large white onion, halved
6 garlic cloves
2 tablespoons kosher salt
1 tablespoon black pepper
2 dried bay leaves
1 teaspoon dried Mexican oregano
1 teaspoon whole cumin seeds
3 whole cloves

1 cup crushed pineapple
2 ounces (56g) achiote paste
¼ cup white distilled vinegar
1 whole pineapple

For serving:
Corn tortillas (for homemade see pages 23 and 24 or store-bought)
Limes wedges
Chopped fresh cilantro
Finely chopped white onion
Pineapple Salsa Verde (see page 55)

special equipment
Mini trompo (optional)

al pastor

serves: **about 4 cups**
prep time: **10 minutes**
cook time: **about 3 hours**
total time: **about 3 hours and 10 minutes (plus marinating time)**

If I had to pick one type of taco to eat for the rest of my life, this would be the one. And if I could only source those tacos from one place for the rest of my life (homemade or store-bought), it would be the al pastor tacos from Taqueria Atotonilco in Chicago. I grew up within walking distance from them and I swear they are the best of the best. But since I haven't lived in Chicago for a while, these are the next best thing. The pork is flavorful and you can use it for more than just tacos. The mini trompo (the contraption traditionally used for stacking the meat) isn't needed (see the Note for an alternative cooking method), but it does work to give you the traditional look of al pastor tacos, especially if you're serving these to a crowd.

If you do not have mini trompo, you can find many on Amazon for as low as $25. You can also cook the marinated pork slices on an outdoor grill for about 4 to 5 minutes per side. Or use a large indoor skillet on medium-high heat. Once cooked, thinly slice or chop it up for tacos.

1   Place the pork shoulder in the freezer for 30 to 45 minutes.

2   While the pork is in the freezer, start preparing the marinade.

3   Add the dried guajillo and ancho peppers to a medium sauce pot with enough water to cover. Bring to a boil, then turn off the heat and let the peppers sit for 10 to 15 minutes to cool down and continue rehydrating.

4   Add the avocado oil, rehydrated chiles, ½ cup of the chile water, half the white onion, garlic cloves, salt, pepper, bay leaves, oregano, cumin seeds, cloves, achiote paste, crushed pineapple, and vinegar to a blender. Blend the ingredients until a smooth paste is formed, 30 to 45 seconds.

5   Thinly slice the remaining half of the onion and set aside.

6   Cut off 1 inch from the top and 1 inch from the bottom of the whole pineapple. Carefully cut the skin off the remaining pineapple and thinly slice it into rounds. The top and bottom pieces of the pineapple will be used to assemble the al pastor trompo.

7   Remove the pork from the freezer and, using a sharp knife, slice it into roughly ¼-inch slices.

8   Once the pork is sliced, using a large bowl or container with a lid, combine the pork with the al pastor marinade. Let the pork marinate for at least 2 hours or up to 8 hours. The longer the better.

9   Once ready to cook, preheat your oven to 300°F (150°C).

10   Start assembling the trompo by placing the bottom part of the pineapple through the skewer.

11   Proceed by layering the marinated pork, sliced onion, and sliced pineapple. Alternate by doing a couple layers of pork then pineapple, and spread out the thinly sliced onions throughout. Finish with the top part of the pineapple as the final item on the skewer.

12   Cover the whole trompo lightly with aluminum foil. Add the trompo to the oven to cook for 2½ hours.

13   Remove the foil, raise the temperature to 350°F (180°) and cook for 45 more minutes.

14   The al pastor is ready to serve when it reaches an internal temperature of 150°F (65°C).

15   Let the al pastor rest about 15 minutes before slicing into it.

16   To serve, use a sharp knife to shave off slices of the al pastor. Serve with tortillas, pineapple salsa verde, freshly chopped onion and cilantro, and a fresh squeeze of lime juice.

learn more about assembling a trompo

For the Picadillo:
1 tablespoon avocado oil
1 pound (453g) ground beef
½ large white onion, finely
    chopped
2 Yukon gold potatoes, cut
    into small cubes
1 tablespoon paprika
1 tablespoon tomato
    chicken bouillon
1 teaspoon onion powder
1 teaspoon garlic powder
1 teaspoon guajillo chile
    powder
1 teaspoon kosher salt
1 teaspoon black pepper

2 garlic cloves, grated
1 bell pepper, diced

For Assembly and Serving:
12 to 16 corn tortillas (for
    homemade see page 24 or
    store-bought)
Oil, for frying
Refried Beans (see page 29)
Shredded cheese
Shredded lettuce
Diced tomatoes
Salsa of choice
Lime wedges
Mexican crema

picadillo

serves: 4
prep time: **10 minutes**
cook time: **45 minutes**
total time: **55 minutes**

These tacos are one of the dishes my mom had on
heavy rotation growing up. We had them a couple
times a month and I absolutely loved them because
she would serve them buffet-style with loads of
toppings to choose from. You must have them with
the homemade fried tortilla shells—sure you can use
store-bought tortilla shells, but they really will not
be the same.

1   Add the oil to a large sauté pan set over medium-high
    heat.

2   Add the ground beef and start breaking it down into
    smaller pieces. Cook for 3 to 4 minutes.

3   Add the onion and potatoes and cook for 5 to 6
    minutes, stirring every minute or so.

4   Add the spices, garlic, and bell pepper, mix to combine
    well, and cook for 4 to 5 minutes.

5   Reduce heat to medium-low, add in ½ cup water, and
    mix around to combine. Cover with a lid and cook for
    10 to 15 minutes or until the potatoes are cooked
    through. Turn off heat.

6   To a large frying pan set over medium heat, add enough
    oil to cover the bottom of the pan with about ¼ inch of
    oil.

7   Once hot, add in a corn tortilla, and using metal tongs,
    grab one side of the tortilla and fold it in half like a taco
    but leave it slightly open. Let the tortilla fry for about 20
    to 30 seconds with half of it folded in the air, then flip
    the side that has been in the air to continue frying for
    another 20 to 30 seconds. Fry each tortilla until it's
    mostly holding its shape.

8   Place the fried tortillas on a paper towel–lined plate to
    absorb any excess oil and continue frying until all the
    shells are made. Season the tortilla shells immediately
    with a sprinkling of salt.

9   To assemble the tacos, spread some refried beans on
    the bottom of the tortilla shell, sprinkle in some cheese,
    and top it off with some of the picadillo.

10 Finish off the tacos with lettuce, tomato, salsa, lime,
    and crema.

**learn more about how to fry
hard shell tacos**

for the tacos:
8 ounces Mexican chorizo
2 tablespoons avocado oil
1× 7 ounce (200g) bag fideo noodles (often labeled as vermicelli)
1 tablespoon tomato chicken bouillon
3 teaspoons guajillo chile powder
1 teaspoon onion powder
1 teaspoon garlic powder
1× 8 ounce (226g) can tomato sauce

3 cups chicken broth or water
12 to 16 corn tortillas (for homemade see page 24 or store-bought)
Cooking oil spray

for serving:
Crumbled queso fresco
Sliced avocado
Mexican crema
Salsa of choice
Lime wedge

tacos de fideo seco

serves: **4 to 6**
prep time: **10 minutes**
cook time: **50 minutes**
total time: **1 hour**

The first time I ever heard of tacos de fideo seco was in a magazine back in 2018. I made them the next day and the rest was history. Okay, maybe I was a bit dramatic there, but these tacos were everything I could've hoped for and something you can easily whip up to impress your friends and family. Serve these chorizo and noodle tacos with a bar of toppings like queso fresco, aguacate, crema, salsa, and limon.

1   Add the chorizo to a large sauté pan set over medium heat. Cook, breaking up into smaller pieces, for about 4 minutes.

2   Add the oil and fideo to the pan and cook, stirring frequently for about 6 minutes.

3   Add the spices, mix to combine, and cook for 2 more minutes.

4   Add the tomato chicken bouillon and chicken broth, reduce the heat to medium-low, and cook, stirring frequently, for 10 to 12 minutes or until most of the broth has cooked through. Turn off the heat.

5   Set a large frying pan or a comal over medium heat.

6   To assemble the tacos, working with 2 to 3 tortillas at a time, spray the comal with oil, then place the tortillas. Heat up for about 30 seconds, flip over, add about ¼ cup of the fideo to one half of the tortilla, fold it closed in half, and spray with a bit more oil to help them get crispy. Keep frying the folded tacos until slightly crisp, about 1 minute per side. Continue assembling tacos, spraying the comal with more oil as needed until you've used up all the fideo.

7   Serve the tacos with your choice of toppings such as crumbled queso fresco, avocado, salsa, Mexican crema, and a fresh squeeze of lime juice.

8 large eggs
⅓ cup mayo, plus more as
  needed
1 avocado, diced
1 jalapeño, finely chopped
¼ small red onion, finely
  chopped
½ cup chopped fresh
  cilantro

Juice of 1 lime
2 teaspoons kosher salt
1 teaspoon black pepper
8 flour tortillas (for
  homemade see page 23 or
  store-bought)
½ cup oil, for frying

guac egg salad tacos

serves: **2 to 4**
prep time: **15 minutes**
cook time: **30 minutes**
total time: **45 minutes**

In recent years I've become a lover of egg salads. When I'm working at home and want an easy lunch, I'll prepare an egg salad with whatever I have on hand because I always have eggs and mayo. One day, my friend Anjelah Johnson-Reyes kept requesting I try making egg salad tacos, and I'm so glad she did because I never would've tried these if it wasn't for her.

1   Set a large sauce pot filled with water over medium-high heat and add in the eggs. Bring the water a boil and let the eggs boil for 8 minutes.

2   Remove the eggs from the boiling water and immediately place them into a bowl of ice water. Peel the eggs and roughly chop them, then add to a large mixing bowl.

3   To the bowl with the chopped boiled eggs, add in the mayo along with the avocado, jalapeño, red onion, cilantro, lime juice, salt, and pepper. Mix well to combine. Taste and adjust any seasonings if needed, or add more mayo if you want (I'm a mayo lover so sometimes I add more than necessary).

4   To assemble the tacos, add ⅓ cup egg salad to each tortilla and roll it up tightly. Continue with the rest of the tortillas and egg salad.

5   Set a large frying pan over medium heat and add the oil. Once the oil is hot, add the rolled-up tacos with the seam-side down. Fry on the first side for 1 to 2 minutes or until golden brown. Flip over and cook for another 1 to 2 minutes or until golden brown all over. Once cooked, place on a paper towel–lined plate to soak up any excess oil.

6   Serve up the tacos and enjoy.

4 calabacitas, or zucchini
2 tablespoons olive oil
1 tablespoon lemon-pepper
  seasoning
1 teaspoon paprika
1 teaspoon garlic powder
1 teaspoon onion powder
1 teaspoon kosher salt
1 teaspoon black pepper

Cooking oil spray
1 pound (453g) Muenster
  cheese or any melting
  cheese, shredded
10 to 12 corn tortillas (for
  homemade see page 24 or
  store-bought)
Pico de Gallo, for serving
  (see page 122)

costra de calabaza

serves: 4
prep time: 5 minutes
cook time: 30 minutes
total time: 35 minutes

It's a funny name, I know (it loosely translates to "something crusty"), but here "costra" refers to the toasty, melty cheese that is covering the tortillas for these tacos. Whenever I'm making tacos with a vegetarian filling, I like to do the crusty cheese on the tortilla to make them even more special. On many occasions, I've had these tacos for dinner because they're super fast to make, but we also always add a couple of these calabazas to the grill when having a carne asada.

1   Cut the ends off of each calabacita, then quarter them to get 4 spears from each.

2   Add the calabacita pieces to a bowl along with the olive oil and all of the spices and mix well to fully coat the pieces.

3   Set a large frying pan over medium heat and spray with oil.

4   Add the calabacita pieces in a single layer, cook for 2 to 3 minutes on one cut side, turn over to the other cut side and cook for another 2 to 3 minutes, and lastly, turn them onto the rounded side and cook for another 2 minutes. Reduce the heat to low while you prepare the tortillas.

5   Set a nonstick comal or skillet over medium heat. Once hot, sprinkle roughly ½ cup of shredded cheese to form a circle onto the pan. Let the cheese melt for about 1 minute or until the bottom part of the cheese is getting golden brown and crispy and top off the melted cheese with a corn tortilla. Flip it over to let the tortilla cook for about 30 to 45 seconds. Continue this process with all the tortillas and cheese.

6   Top off each costra with one or two pieces of calabacitas and serve with Pico de Gallo.

4 to 5 pounds (1¾ to 2 kg)
  pork belly
Cooking oil spray

for the marinade:
1 cup kimchi, plus more for
  serving
¼ cup gochujang
¼ cup rice vinegar
1 small white onion,
  roughly chopped
5 garlic cloves
1 tablespoon gochugaru
  pepper flakes
¼ cup soy sauce

1 teaspoon toasted sesame
  oil
1 tablespoon kosher salt

for serving:
Corn or flour tortillas (for
  homemade see pages 23
  and 24 or store-bought)
Kimchi Pico de Gallo (see
  page 60)
Sriracha

special equipment
Blender

pork belly kimchi tacos

serves: **4 to 6**
prep time: **15 minutes**
cook time: **45 minutes**
total time: **1 hour (plus marinating time)**

It's hard not to love pork belly—it's meaty, fatty, and delicious. This marinated pork belly comes together so quickly and easily that you'll be mad at yourself for never cooking it like this until now. There is a misconception out there that pork belly is extremely difficult to cook, but by dicing and marinating it, we can cook it in a hot skillet in less than 10 minutes.

1   Place the pork belly in the freezer for 30 minutes so it'll firm up and make it easier to cut.

2   Cut up the pork belly into smaller chunks—don't worry about having them all be the exact same size. Add the cut-up pork belly into a large plastic zip-top bag.

3   Add the marinade ingredients to your blender and blend until smooth and combined.

4   Pour the marinade over the pork belly in the plastic bag, close it up, and mix around, making sure all the pieces are fully coated.

5   If possible, marinate the pork belly for up to 8 hours or overnight, but you can also refrigerate and marinate for at least 1 hour.

6   When ready to cook the meat, set a large, nonstick sauté pan over medium-high heat and spray with oil to cover the pan.

7   Once hot, start cooking the pork belly in batches, mixing the pieces around every 2 minutes or so. Cook the pork belly for about 8 minutes total or until parts of it are getting slightly charred and caramelized. Remove from the pan and continue cooking the rest of the pork belly, adding more spray oil as needed, until all the pork belly has been cooked through.

8   To serve, in the same pan we cooked the pork belly in, heat up the tortillas for about 20 to 30 seconds per side.

9   Serve the tacos with some of the cooked pork belly, sriracha, and Kimchi Pico de Gallo.

Cooking the pork belly in batches makes it easier to get crispy pork belly pieces instead of having it steam while cooking.

2 pounds (900g) New York Strip Steak or any steak, thinly sliced

for the gochujang-lime sauce:
½ cup gochujang
2 tablespoons sriracha
1 tablespoon gochugaru
1 tablespoon soy sauce
Juice of 1 to 2 limes (start with 1 lime, but if it doesn't have much juice, use 2)

for the bulgogi:
1 Asian pear, core removed and quartered
1 small onion, quartered
5 garlic cloves
2-inch piece ginger

3 tablespoons brown sugar
¼ cup soy sauce
2 tablespoons mirin
1 tablespoon toasted sesame oil
2 teaspoons kosher salt
1 jalapeño, stem removed and sliced into thin rounds
Oil for cooking

for serving:
Corn Tortillas (for homemade see page 24 or store-bought)
4 green onions, thinly sliced
Pickled Red Onions (see page 51)
Toasted sesame seeds

bulgogi tacos

serves: **4**
prep time: **15 minutes**
cook time: **45 minutes**
total time: **1 hour (plus marinating time)**

If I am at a Korean restaurant, I am 1,000% getting bulgogi (and then every other dish on the menu, but bulgogi for sure). There are many ways to make it, but it's always a bit sweet or with a little bit of spice—or both sweet and spicy. I simply love everything about it. And since bulgogi is marinated beef, I knew I had to make tacos out of bulgogi. And boy am I glad I did, because these are incredible and you, too, must make them!

1 Make the sauce by adding all the ingredients into a mixing bowl, stir to combine, taste, and add any salt to taste. Refrigerate until ready to use.

2 Add the steaks to the freezer while you prepare the marinade—you want them slightly chilled so they're easier to slice.

3 To make the marinade, add the pear, onion, garlic, ginger, brown sugar, soy sauce, mirin, toasted sesame oil, and salt to a blender. Blend until fully combined.

4 Remove the steak from the freezer and slice it as thinly as you can. Once sliced, add it to a large bowl.

5 Pour the blended marinade into the meat and mix it up, making sure all the meat is fully coated. Cover and let marinate in the fridge for at least 30 minutes, but up to 6 hours if you can.

6 When you're ready to cook the meat, take out the gochujang-lime sauce so it comes to room temperature, and take out the meat as well.

7 Set a large sauté pan over medium-high heat and add 1 tablespoon of oil.

8 Once the pan is hot, add in about ¼ of the marinated beef. We are cooking it in batches so the meat cooks faster and we can more easily get a nice sear and char all over. Spread out the meat into an even single layer, top with some of the sliced jalapeño, and cook undisturbed for 4 minutes.

9 After 4 minutes, start mixing around in the pan and cook for an additional 3 to 4 minutes or until the meat is cooked through and charred in parts. Remove the cooked meat and place it in a serving bowl. Continue cooking the rest of the meat in batches, adding oil to the pan as needed.

10 To serve, warm up corn tortillas in the same skillet that the meat was cooked in on medium heat for about 20 to 30 seconds per side.

11 Add some of the cooked meat to each tortilla, along with some of the sauce, pickled red onions, sesame seeds, and thinly sliced green onions.

8 to 10 jalapeños, try to get the biggest ones you can find

8 ounces (226g) Muenster cheese

½× 8 ounce (226g) block cream cheese

10 to 12 slices thin-cut bacon, plus more as needed

for serving:
10 corn tortillas (for homemade see page 24 or store-bought)
Pico de Gallo (see page 122)

special equipment
Air fryer (optional)

jalapeño popper tacos

makes: **8 to 10 tacos**
prep time: **20 minutes**
cook time: **40 minutes**
total time: **1 hour**

If you invite me to a carne asada and you have bacon-wrapped jalapeños on the grill, the first thing I'm going to eat is a taco filled with a jalapeño popper and topped with salsa and pico de gallo. I love eating them like this so much that I came up with an air-fried version that I can make whenever I'm craving these tacos.

1 Prepare the jalapeños by carefully making a T-shaped cut from the stem down to the tip, making sure not to cut all the way through.

2 Using a small spoon, carefully open the jalapeños and remove as many of the seeds as you can.

3 Cut both the Muenster cheese and cream cheese into long planks that you can easily fit into the jalapeños.

4 Stuff the jalapeños with 1 strip each of muenster cheese and cream cheese, and close them back up.

5 Preheat the air fryer or oven to 375°F (190°C) degrees.

6 Wrap up the jalapeños with the bacon (use 2 slices if you need to fully cover them). To avoid using toothpicks, I wrap them up to the point where both ends of the bacon are facing down when the popper is on the table.

7 Cover the bottom of a sheet tray with aluminum foil and place the jalapeño poppers on top.

8 Air fry or bake for 20 to 25 minutes.

9 Set the cooked poppers onto a paper towel–lined plate immediately after cooking to soak up any of the excess bacon grease.

10 On your comal or large nonstick pan set over medium heat, warm up the corn tortillas for 20 to 30 seconds per side.

11 Serve the tacos with one popper per taco and top it off with pico de gallo.

Avoid overstuffing the jalapeños with cheese or else it will all ooze out when cooking.

You can use toothpicks to hold the bacon ends in place, please just remember to remove them before serving.

sandwiches

Taki's chicken sandwich.............104

sweet & spicy coconut lobster
(or shrimp) sandwich................106

spicy mortadella sandwich...... 107

chipotle avocado blt..................109

sloppy jose's...................................110

mexican smash burgers 113

chilaquiles burger 114

for the chicken:
4 to 6 boneless skinless
 chicken thighs
1½ cups buttermilk
1 tablespoon paprika
1 tablespoon Tajín
1 teaspoon onion powder
1 teaspoon garlic powder
1 teaspoon black pepper
1 teaspoon kosher salt
¼ teaspoon ground
 cayenne pepper

for the breading:
1 cup all-purpose flour
4 to 5 cups Takis, any
 flavor, finely crushed
1 teaspoon paprika
1 teaspoon onion powder
1 teaspoon garlic powder
1 teaspoon kosher salt
1 teaspoon black pepper
Oil, for frying

for assembly:
4 sandwich rolls
Mayonnaise
Cheese slices (pepper jack
 or Muenster)
Lettuce/tomatoes/pickles

Takis chicken sandwich

makes: **4 sandwiches**
prep time: **none**
cook time: **1 hour**
total time: **1 hour (plus marinating time)**

You just can't go wrong with a juicy piece of chicken
fried to crispy perfection sandwiched between two
pieces of bread. I always crave a good chicken
sandwich, so using Takis as the "bread crumbs" was
a no-brainer. Frying chicken may seem intimidating,
but by using chicken thighs we ensure the chicken
will be juicy without having to worry about
overcooking it.

1 To marinate the chicken, add the chicken thighs to a
   large mixing bowl. Add all the seasonings and the
   buttermilk. Mix to combine and let marinate at room
   temperature for at least 30 minutes, or 4 to 6 hours in
   the refrigerator.

2 To prepare the dredging station, get 2 large paper
   plates or disposable aluminum baking trays. To the first
   one, add the flour and the seasonings, and to the other,
   add the crushed-up Takis.

3 Start breading the chicken thighs by removing them all
   from the buttermilk mixture, letting any excess drip off.
   Set them aside on a plate, don't throw the marinade
   away yet.

4 Pass the chicken through the flour mixture, back
   through the remaining buttermilk mixture, then
   through the crushed-up Takis, making sure the chicken
   is fully coated all over.

5 Set the coated chicken on a baking sheet and continue
   breading the rest of the chicken.

6 To a large frying pan set over medium-high heat, add
   enough oil to cover the pan with about 1 inch of oil.

7 Once the oil is hot, start frying the chicken 2 pieces at a
   time to avoid overcrowding the pan. Fry the chicken for
   3 to 4 minutes on the first side. Flip over and fry for
   another 3 to 4 minutes on the other side.

8 Once the chicken is crispy all over and cooked through
   with an internal temperature of 165°F (75°C), place it on
   a paper towel–lined plate to soak up any excess oil.

9 Immediately top the fried chicken with a slice of cheese
   so the carryover heat can help melt it.

10 To assemble the chicken sandwich, slather your
   sandwich rolls with mayo, add the lettuce on the
   bottom bun followed by one piece of chicken, and top
   off the chicken with pickles, tomatoes, and the top
   piece of bread.

11 Slice in half and enjoy!

for the sauce:
2 habanero peppers, halved and deseeded (see note)
1 cup sour cream
1 cup crushed pineapple
½ cup sweetened condensed milk
Zest and juice of 1 lime
1 teaspoon salt

for the coconut lobster:
4 lobster tails, thawed if frozen

1 cup all-purpose flour
1 teaspoon garlic powder
1 teaspoon salt, plus more for sprinkling
1 teaspoon black pepper
2 eggs
½ cup whole milk
1 cup panko bread crumbs
2 cups sweetened coconut flakes
Oil for frying, preferably coconut oil
4 brioche burger buns

sweet & spicy coconut lobster (or shrimp) sandwich

makes: **4 sandwiches**
prep time: **20 minutes**
cook time: **40 minutes**
total time: **1 hour**

In 2023, Royal Caribbean invited me on a cruise. One of the stops was Coco Cay, their private island, and in the beach club they have this beauty of a coconut lobster sandwich. After the first bite, I immediately fell in love. I knew then and there that I'd be making my own version at home. My version is not identical to the original, but it's pretty darn good. It's sweet from the coconut breading and the creamy pineapple sauce, but also slightly spicy from the hint of habanero pepper thrown in. Lobster can be pretty pricey, so feel free to sub the largest shrimp you can find for a slightly thriftier option.

Use food-safe plastic gloves to handle the habanero pepper. This will keep your hands from getting burned.

If using shrimp, look for the biggest shrimp you can find, coat them the exact same way, cook for 2 to 3 minutes per side, and use 3 to 4 shrimp per sandwich.

1 Add all of the sauce ingredients to a medium bowl and mix to combine. Taste and add any additional salt as needed. Refrigerate until ready to serve.

2 Using kitchen scissors, carefully make a lengthwise cut along the underside of the lobster tail shells, then carefully use the opening to remove the lobster tails from the shells.

3 Once you have the lobster tails out, cut them down the middle, making sure not to cut through, and open them like a book.

4 Prepare the dredging station using three different sheet pans: to the first, add the flour, garlic powder, salt, and pepper. To the second sheet pan, add the 2 eggs and whole milk and whisk to combine. To the third sheet pan, add the panko bread crumbs and coconut flakes and mix to combine.

5 Coat the lobster tails by passing them first through the flour mixture, making sure they are coated all over. Then pass them through the egg wash mixture, making sure to coat all over. And lastly, pass them through the coconut-panko mixture, making sure to pat them to fully coat all over.

6 To a large frying pan set over medium heat, add enough oil to cover the pan with about ½ inch of oil.

7 Once hot, fry the lobster tails until golden brown and crispy, 3 to 4 minutes on the first side and 3 to 4 minutes on the second side.

8 Place the cooked lobster tails on a paper towel–lined baking sheet to soak up any excess oil and immediately season with salt.

9 To serve, toast up the buns on a dry skillet for 15 to 20 seconds per side over medium heat. Slather both sides of the buns with the sauce and fill the sandwiches with one lobster tail per bun.

for the jalapeño mayo:
⅓ cup mayonnaise
2 pickled jalapeños, finely chopped
1 tablespoon jalapeño pickling liquid
½ teaspoon kosher salt

for the sandwiches:
½ pound mortadella, thinly sliced
2 slices Muenster cheese
2 sandwich rolls
Dijon mustard
Giardiniera, for serving

spicy mortadella sandwich

makes: **2 sandwiches**
prep time: **5 minutes**
cook time: **25 minutes**
total time: **30 minutes**

The late, great Anthony Bourdain shared a version of this recipe in his cookbook *Appetites.* By now I have lost count of how many times I've made it. This is my take on the sandwich with a spicy twist, of course. It's simple yet packs so much flavor—you'll be craving it every day.

1   Add all ingredients for the mayo to a small bowl and mix to combine. Taste and adjust seasonings as needed. Refrigerate until ready to assemble.

2   Set a large frying pan over medium heat.

3   Form mounds of the thinly sliced mortadella by irregularly folding slices of mortadella on top of each other, forming two mortadella patties.

4   Place each mortadella mountain on the hot skillet, cook for 2 to 3 minutes on the first side, flip over, place a slice of cheese on each mortadella patty, and cook for another 2 to 3 minutes.

5   Remove the mortadella from the pan and in the same pan toast up the sandwich rolls on both sides for about 20 to 30 seconds per side.

6   To assemble the sandwiches, spread some of the jalapeño mayo on both sides of the bread, add about 1 teaspoon of mustard to the bottom bun, and spread it.

7   Lay the cooked mortadella on the bottom bun, top it off with a spoonful or two of giardiniera, and close up the sandwich with the top roll.

for the sandwiches:
8 slices thick-cut bacon
4 slices sandwich bread
1 Roma tomato, sliced
1 avocado, sliced
Romaine lettuce, leaves
  separated and cut in half
  crosswise

for the chipotle mayo:
1 cup mayonnaise
3 tablespoons chipotle
  sauce
1 teaspoon kosher salt
½ teaspoon black pepper
½ teaspoon paprika
½ teaspoon garlic powder
½ teaspoon onion powder
½ teaspoon guajillo chile
  powder
Juice of 1 lime

chipotle avocado blt

makes: **2 sandwiches**
prep time: **5 minutes**
cook time: **25 minutes**
total time: **30 minutes**

One of my favorite sandwiches ever is the BLT, it's so simple but when done right it could be the best thing you'll eat that day. You probably already have everything in your kitchen to make it. And you'll want to use this spicy chipotle mayo for literally everything.

1   Preheat the oven to 375°F (190°C).

2   Lay out the bacon on a baking sheet and cook until crispy, 16 to 20 minutes.

3   While the bacon cooks make the chipotle mayo by adding all the ingredients to a small mixing bowl. Stir to combine. Taste and adjust any seasonings as needed. Refrigerate until ready to use.

4   In your toaster or on your comal set over medium heat, toast the bread to your desired doneness.

5   Once the bacon is ready, briefly put it on a paper towel–lined plate to soak up any excess fat.

6   To assemble the sandwiches, slather one side of each slice of bread with the chipotle mayo. Lay out the lettuce on one side and the avocado on the other. Top the lettuce with 3 to 4 slices of bacon and top the bacon with the sliced tomatoes.

7   Slice in half and enjoy.

½ pound (226g) ground beef
½ pound (226g) chorizo, preferably beef
1 small white onion, finely chopped
1 bell pepper, chopped
1 teaspoon garlic powder
1 teaspoon kosher salt
1 teaspoon black pepper
½ teaspoon ground cumin
1 cup tomato sauce
½ cup Enchilada Sauce, (see page 147)
¼ cup chipotle sauce
4 burger buns
Crumbled queso fresco
Sliced avocado

sloppy jose's

serves: 4
prep time: **5 minutes**
cook time: **25 minutes**
total time: **30 minutes**

Sloppy joes are one of the American foods I never really loved and would only have when it was offered in elementary school for lunch. But one day, I had so much extra enchilada sauce and boom, I was inspired to make my own Mexican version of a sloppy joe. They're saucy and delicious, and they come together so fast for an easy dinner.

1 To a large sauté pan set over medium heat, add the ground beef and chorizo. Break it down into smaller pieces as it cooks for 5 to 6 minutes.

2 Add in the diced onion, bell pepper, and spices. Mix and cook for 4 to 6 more minutes or until the onion has started to soften.

3 Add the tomato sauce, enchilada sauce, and chipotle sauce and mix to combine. Reduce the heat to low and let it simmer for 12 to 15 minutes. Turn off the heat, taste, and adjust any seasonings as needed.

4 To serve, you can toast the buns (if you'd like), then top the bottom of each bun with some of the sloppy jose mixture and finish it with crumbled queso fresco and slices of avocado.

You can use all ground beef if you don't want to use chorizo.

10 to 12 slices thin bacon
1 small white onion, thinly
    sliced
4 slices ham
1 pound ground beef
Kosher salt and black
    pepper, to taste
4 slices American cheese
4 slices Muenster cheese

for serving:
4 hamburger buns
Mayonnaise
Ketchup
Yellow mustard
Tomato slices
Dill pickle chips
Lettuce
Mashed avocado
Sliced pickled jalapeños

mexican smash burgers

makes: **4 burgers**
prep time: **10 minutes**
cook time: **50 minutes**
total time: **1 hour**

Mexican burgers are so good because they're more than just a beef patty with cheese—they'll have seared ham, bacon, and sometimes even a fried egg and seared slices of pineapple. There are so many ways to make them but this is my go-to method. It's gotta have the ham, but when it comes to the rest of the toppings, feel free to sub/change for whatever you like most.

To keep the bacon and ham warm, you can place them on your comal on the lowest heat setting possible and as close to the edges as possible.

If you don't want to put the sliced pickled jalapeños in the burger, you can leave them whole and serve them on the side.

You can use only one of the cheeses if you don't want to use both.

1 Set a large frying pan over medium-high heat and cook the bacon until crispy, 6 to 8 minutes, flipping as needed.

2 Drain off any of the excess fat, leaving about 1 tablespoon in the pan. Reduce the heat to medium, add the thinly sliced onions, and cook them for 8 to 10 minutes or until just starting to soften and brown a bit. Remove onions from the pan and set aside.

3 In the same pan, sear the slices of ham for 1 minute per side. Remove the ham from the pan and set aside.

4 Divide the ground beef into 4 balls and season them with salt and pepper.

5 In the same skillet over medium heat, add the burger patties, and using a large spatula, flatten them out to your desired thickness. Cook for 3 to 4 minutes on the first side, flip them over, top with 1 slice each of the Muenster and American cheese, and cook for 2 to 3 more minutes. Turn off the heat and cover with a lid to keep warm and to help the cheese melt.

6 Set a comal or nonstick skillet over medium heat, slather a bit of mayo on both sides of the burger buns, and toast them for 30 to 45 seconds per side.

7 Assemble the burgers by spreading more mayonnaise on the buns, followed by ketchup and mustard on the bottom bun. Top it with the burger patty and put a slice of ham on top of the patty, followed by the bacon, tomatoes, pickles, pickled jalapeños, and lettuce. Slather mashed avocado on the top buns, close up the burgers, and enjoy.

learn how to make simple
homemade guacamole

for the burgers:
2 pounds (907g) ground beef
Kosher salt and black pepper, to taste
6 corn tortillas (for homemade see page 24 or store-bought), cut into small squares

½ cup oil for frying
8 slices Muenster cheese
4 eggs
1 avocado, sliced
4 hamburger buns
Mayonnaise
Mexican crema
Salsa verde (see page 50)

chilaquiles burger

makes: **4 burgers**
prep time: **10 minutes**
cook time: **1 hour**
total time: **1 hour and 10 minutes**

Recently it's seemed like people will add anything to a burger and call it a day, so why not add chilaquiles as a topping? I've been playing around with the idea of a chilaquiles burger for a while and when I finally figured it out, I was mad for not doing it sooner. It just simply works. Make it for brunch or dinner. I prefer mine with salsa verde, but you can also use salsa roja. Also don't forget the egg, it's a must!

This makes 4 large burger patties. You can make them smaller if you like by using ¼ lb meat per patty instead of ½ lb.

The smaller you cut the tortilla squares, the better. This is a messy buger regardless, but the smaller squares will help to tamp down the mess factor slightly.

1 In a large frying pan set to medium-high heat add in the oil.

2 Once hot, add in the cut-up tortilla pieces and fry, stirring frequently until golden brown and crispy, about 6 to 8 minutes.

3 Transfer the tortilla pieces to a paper towel–lined plate to drain off the excess oil.

4 Form the burger patties by separating the ground beef into 4 patties, about ½ pound (226g) each. Season all over with salt and pepper.

5 Remove excess oil from the frying pan and save it for later. Return the pan to the burner and set to medium-high heat. Once hot, add the burger patties, and cook for 3 to 4 minutes on the first side. Flip over and cook for 3 to 4 more minutes. Flip once more and cook for 2 more minutes.

6 Turn off the heat, top off with one slice of cheese, and cover with a lid. Leave covered until ready to assemble.

7 In another nonstick skillet, add 1 to 2 tablespoons of the oil used to crisp up the tortilla pieces, set to medium heat, and fry the eggs to your liking. Remove and set aside.

8 Toast the burger buns on the same pan. I like to slather the cut sides with about 1 tablespoon of mayo before toasting. Toast for 1 to 2 minutes per side.

9 Assemble your burger by drizzling Mexican crema on the bottom bun, then adding the burger Add a handful of the crispy tortilla chips on top of the patty, spoon over the salsa verde, about ¼ cup, and immediately add another slice of cheese on top of the salsa. You can let the cheese melt with the carryover heat from the salsa or briefly place it under the broiler to fully melt the cheese.

10 Finish off the burger with slices of avocado, the fried egg, and another drizzle of Mexican crema.

11 Place the top bun, smash it down a bit to break the yolk, and enjoy.

the carne asada

carne asada 2 ways 118

carne asada matrix 120

pico de gallo 122

watermelon feta salad 123

elote potato salad 126

pollo asado 129

carne asada
two ways

serves: **6 to 8**
prep time: **10 minutes**
cook time: **30 minutes**
total time: **40 minutes (plus marinating time)**

Carne asada is a recipe, but it's also the act of coming together with family and friends to enjoy good food with good company. When it comes to the main attraction, there are two ways of preparing the carne asada: simply with salt and pepper or all-out with tons of ingredients in the marinade. Whichever route you decide to go, you won't be disappointed.

salt & pepper way:
6 to 8 pounds (2¾ to 3½ kg) skirt steak or flank steak
2 tablespoons kosher salt
1 tablespoon black pepper, plus more to taste

marinated way:
6 to 8 pounds (2¾ to 3½ kg) skirt steak or flank steak
2 tablespoons seasoned salt or kosher salt
1 tablespoon black pepper
Juice of 2 limes
Juice of 2 oranges
1× 12 ounce (355 ml) can of light beer, such as Miller Lite or Modelo
¼ cup avocado oil
2 teaspoons garlic powder
1 large white onion, thinly sliced
1 bunch cilantro

for serving:
Tortillas of choice
Desired sides and salsas

1   If cooking with salt and pepper, season the steak all over with the salt and pepper.

2   If marinating the steak, season all over with the seasoned salt and pepper.

3   In a measuring cup add the lime juice, orange juice, can of beer, oil, and garlic powder, and stir to combine.

4   In a large bowl or disposable aluminum container, layer the steak, pour over some of the marinade, and scatter around the thinly sliced onion. Continue to layer the steak with the rest of the marinade and the cilantro and onion. Marinate for at least 2 hours and up to 8 hours.

5   When ready to cook, fire up the grill. Once hot, start cooking the steak. Depending on your desired doneness (I usually go for medium rare), cook the steak for 4 to 5 minutes per side. If you want a more well-done steak, cook for 7 to 8 minutes per side. Set on a cutting board and let rest for 10 to 15 minutes before slicing.

6   Slice up and serve with tortillas and your favorite sides and salsas.

The simplest way to use your carne asada is for tacos, but there are so many other things you can make with it, and these are just a few of those ways. None of these recipes have set measurements, they are meant to be quick and dirty.

Hot dogs
Bacon
Carne Asada (see page 118)
Hot dog buns
Mayonnaise
Mustard
Ketchup
Pico de Gallo (see page 122)

Frozen French fries
Cooking oil spray
Carne Asada (see page 118)
Canned nacho cheese
Guacamole
Pico de Gallo (see page 122)
Queso fresco
Mexican crema
Salsa of choice
Pickled Red Onions (see page 51)

mexican hot dogs

Wrap the hot dogs in bacon and air fry at 375°F (190°C) until the bacon is crispy all over. Meanwhile, dice up the carne asada and warm through in a skillet set over medium heat. Toast the buns, slather with mayo, add the hot dogs, top off with ketchup and mustard. Spoon over some of the carne asada and pico de Gallo.

carne asada fries

Add the frozen French fries to a sheet pan and spray with oil, air fry at 375°F (190°C) until crispy, about 15 minutes. Meanwhile, dice up the carne asada and warm through in a skillet set over medium heat. Warm up the canned nacho cheese in the microwave. When the fries are done, top with nacho cheese, then the diced carne asada, guacamole, pico de gallo, crumbled queso fresco, salsa, and pickled red onions.

carne asada
matrix

Russet potatoes
Oil of choice
Carne Asada (see page 118)
Butter
Canned nacho cheese
Pico de Gallo (see page 122)

〰〰〰〰〰〰〰〰〰〰〰〰〰〰〰〰〰〰

loaded papa asada

Poke the potatoes all over with a fork, coat in oil, and place on a baking sheet. Bake at 400°F (200°C) for 45 to 60 minutes or until the potatoes are fork-tender. Meanwhile, dice up the carne asada and warm through in a skillet set over medium heat. Cut a slit down the middle of the potatoes, open them up and mash up some of the potato with a couple tablespoons of butter. Warm up the nacho cheese in the microwave and pour some into the potato, top it off with the carne asada and pico de gallo.

Teleras or Bolillos
Mayonnaise
Carne Asada (see page 118)
Refried Beans (see page 29)
Shredded Chihuahua cheese
Shredded lettuce
Sliced tomatoes
Mexican Crema
Salsa of choice
Lime wedges

〰〰〰〰〰〰〰〰〰〰〰〰〰〰〰〰〰〰

tortas

Dice up the carne asada and warm it up in a skillet set over medium heat. Slice open the telera, slather both sides with mayonnaise and toast up on your comal over medium heat for about 1 minute per side. Slather warmed up refried beans on the bottom bread, top it off with some of the carne asada, a sprinkling of the shredded cheese, and finish it up with lettuce, tomatoes, crema, salsa, and lime juice.

5 to 6 Roma tomatoes
1 small white onion, finely
  chopped
2 jalapeños, finely
  chopped
1 bunch cilantro, chopped

Juice of 2 limes
1 teaspoon Lawry's
  Seasoned Salt
1 teaspoon black pepper
1 tablespoon Tajin or
  chile-lime seasoning

pico de gallo

makes: **about 5 cups**
prep time: **10 minutes**
cook time: **none**
total time: **10 minutes**

In my family, I think we may take pico de gallo more seriously than we should. It's the perfect start to every single carne asada or party. It's also the one salsa/dip we must make a TON of because we have certain members of the family that will eat it up with a spoon like soup if given the opportunity. Heck, sometimes I have to hide it in the fridge until everyone has arrived at the carne asada or else there won't be any left by the time the rest of the food is ready.

1   Add all the ingredients to a large mixing bowl. Mix to combine.

2   Taste and adjust any seasonings as needed.

3   Serve at your carne asada with chips.

Pico de gallo is one of those recipes that I have probably never made the exact same way more than once. I'll use different seasonings every time, such as just salt and pepper, lemon pepper, etc.

Another thing I will add is diced avocado right before serving.

for the dressing:
3 tablespoons salsa macha
Juice of 2 limes
2 tablespoons olive oil
3 tablespoons honey
1 garlic clove, grated
½ teaspoon dried Mexican
   oregano
1 teaspoon kosher salt
1 teaspoon black pepper

for the salad:
2 English cucumbers or 5
   mini cucumbers, cut into
   half-moons
4 to 5 cups cubed
   watermelon
8 ounces (226g) feta, cubed
2 green onions, thinly sliced
½ cup roughly chopped
   fresh cilantro

watermelon feta salad

serves: **4 to 6**
prep time: **15 minutes**
cook time: **15 minutes**
total time: **30 minutes**

Feta cheese is high up there as one of my favorite cheeses of all time. I could snack on it every single day. I'd always heard how feta and watermelon were a great combination, but I'd never tried it until I whipped up a version of this salad for the photo shoot for my salsa macha campaign. It was love at first sight. It's perfect in every way.

1   To make the dressing, add all ingredients to a measuring cup or mason jar, stir to combine, taste, and adjust any ingredients as needed. Set aside.

2   To assemble the salad, scatter the cucumber, watermelon, and feta all over a serving tray or large bowl.

3   Drizzle the dressing over the salad.

4   Garnish with the sliced green onions and cilantro.

 learn more about salsa macha

2 pounds (907g) baby potatoes

Kosher salt

4 ears of corn, husked, or 2 cups corn kernels, canned or frozen (thawed if frozen)

1 cup mayo

½ cup sour cream

Juice of 2 limes

1 jalapeño, seeds removed (if desired) and finely diced

1 tablespoon Tajín or any chile-lime seasoning, plus more for garnish

1 cup cotija cheese, crumbled, plus more for garnish

1 teaspoon black pepper

1 teaspoon garlic powder

1 teaspoon onion salt

½ cup chopped fresh cilantro, plus more for garnish

◇◇

elote potato salad

serves: **6 to 8**
prep time: **10 minutes**
cook time: **40 minutes**
total time: **50 minutes**

Elotes (or more traditionally known as esquites or street corn here in the States) is one of my all-time favorite snacks. Some days I've even made myself a lazy version of elotes and called it dinner. I love to take the idea and ingredients used in elotes to prepare them in a different, more filling, way. Here I made a potato salad that is sure to become your new favorite. Everyone loves potatoes but mixing them with corn, mayo, cotija cheese, and lime takes them to the next level.

1   Wash and rinse the potatoes. If some are too big, you can cut them in half.

2   Add them to a large pot, cover them with water, and heavily salt the water—this will season the potatoes while cooking.

3   Bring to a boil and cook until the potatoes are fork-tender, 10 to 12 minutes. Drain and set aside.

4   Cook the corn on the cob by either grilling it until charred all over, or by placing it in your air fryer at 375°F (190°C) for 8 to 10 minutes, rotating halfway through.

5   Once slightly cooled, cut the corn off the cob.

6   In a large mixing bowl, add the corn, mayo, sour cream, lime juice, jalapeño, Tajín, cotija cheese, pepper, garlic powder, onion salt, and the chopped cilantro.

7   Mix to combine, and once combined, add in the cooked potatoes. Mix once more, taste, and adjust seasonings as needed.

8   Serve warm or at room temperature

◇◇

For a crispy potato salad, once you have boiled the potatoes, add them to a baking sheet, coat them in olive oil, and roast or air fry until the potatoes are crispy.

1 cup mayonnaise
2 tablespoons paprika
1 tablespoon Tajín or chile-lime seasoning
1 teaspoon cumin
1 teaspoon onion powder
1 teaspoon garlic powder
1 teaspoon guajillo chile powder

2 teaspoons kosher salt
1 teaspoon black pepper
¼ cup diced chipotle peppers in adobo
3 to 4 pounds (1 to 2 kg) boneless skinless chicken thighs or breasts

pollo asado

serves: **4 to 6**
prep time: **10 minutes**
cook time: **50 minutes**
total time: **1 hour (plus marinating time)**

Every carne asada obviously has its fair share of well, carne asada, but it also needs its fair share of pollo asado. For as long as I can remember, my mom has been using mayonnaise as the main ingredient for marinating chicken that we're going to grill. The mayonnaise ensures that your chicken will remain moist no matter what, including even white meat, which is notorious for being dry. I prefer to make this recipe with chicken thighs, but you certainly can use chicken breasts, or use a combination of the two.

1   In a big mixing bowl, add all the ingredients except the chicken. Mix them well to combine.

2   Add the chicken thighs and mix to combine, making sure they are fully coated.

3   Cover the bowl with a lid or plastic wrap and place it in the fridge to marinate for at least 2 hours or up to overnight.

4   When ready to cook, remove the chicken from the fridge.

5   Get your grill nice and hot. Once hot, start cooking the chicken in batches as needed.

6   Cook the chicken thighs for 4 to 5 minutes on the first side.

7   Flip over and cook for another 4 to 5 minutes. Continue with all chicken until complete.

8   Let the chicken cool for 5 minutes before slicing and serving.

If using chicken breasts, cut them in half lengthwise to make cutlets so they aren't too thick and can cook faster.

You can also make this indoors using a large frying pan set over medium-high heat. Cook the chicken for about 4 to 5 minutes per side.

weeknight dinners

macha peanut noodles 132

green spaghetti.............................135

street corn ravioli 136

chori-queso baked spaghetti.......139

mexican lasagna 140

chiles rellenos 143

spinach artichoke quesadillas.....144

enchiladas rojas.............................147

tex-mex enchiladas.......................148

cheeseburger flautas 151

milanesa de res 152

chipotle chicken 153

cilantro lime roast chicken 154

mexican chicken parm 157

poblano pot pie.............................158

chile-lime poke bowls...................161

1 packet ramen noodles
1 tablespoon salsa macha, plus more for serving
1 garlic clove, grated
2 tablespoons creamy peanut butter
1 tablespoon soy sauce
¼ teaspoon toasted sesame oil
1 tablespoon honey, plus more to taste, if desired

serve with:
Crushed peanuts
Cilantro
Thinly sliced green onion
Sesame seeds

macha peanut noodles

serves: **1**
prep time: **5 minutes**
cook time: **20 minutes**
total time: **25 minutes**

This is one of those recipes I'll make when I'm hungry enough to want something, but not hungry enough to warrant a full meal. It only serves one but you can easily scale it up to serve more. Reserve the packet of seasoning from whatever ramen you're using for another time—we'll be using our own seasoning here.

1   Fill a saucepan with enough water to cover the ramen noodles, set it over medium-high heat and bring it to a boil. Once boiling, add the ramen noodles and cook according to the package instructions.

2   While the noodles are cooking, in a frying pan set over medium heat add the salsa macha and the garlic. Stir and cook for 1 minute.

3   Add the peanut butter, soy sauce, sesame oil, and honey, stir to combine and cook for 2 to 3 minutes.

4   Drain the ramen noodles, reserving 1 cup of cooking water. Add the ramen noodles to the frying pan with ½ cup of the reserved water and mix everything well to combine. Add more water as needed until you get your desired consistency.

5   Serve up the ramen noodles with crushed peanuts, more salsa macha, cilantro, thinly sliced green onions and a sprinkling of sesame seeds.

learn more about salsa macha

2 tablespoons kosher salt
1 pound (450g) spaghetti
2 tablespoons avocado oil
1 small white onion, roughly chopped
4 garlic cloves
4 poblano peppers, roasted, peeled, seeds and stems removed (see page 16)
1× 8 ounce (226g) block cream cheese, at room temperature
1 cup Mexican crema or sour cream

1 cup heavy cream
1 tablespoon chicken bouillon
10 ounces (283g) baby spinach
½ cup cilantro, roughly chopped
4 tablespoons unsalted butter
Queso fresco, for garnish

special equipment
Blender

green spaghetti

serves: 4
prep time: 5 minutes
cook time: 30 minutes
total time: 35 minutes

Green spaghetti is a classic in South Texas where I live. If you go to a party, there is a 99% chance they'll be serving green spaghetti. It's easy to make, addictive, and you can pair it with whatever protein you like. Make it once and you'll be making it over and over again because it's that good. And you won't feel too guilty eating multiple servings because I like to sneak a ton of spinach into the sauce.

1   Bring a large pot of water to a boil. Once boiling, add the salt to the water along with the spaghetti. Cook for 1 to 2 minutes less than what the package instructions say. Drain and set aside, making sure to save some of the pasta water.

2   To a large sauté pan over medium heat, add the oil. Once hot, add the onion and garlic and cook for 4 to 5 minutes or until the onion begins to soften.

3   To a blender, add the poblano peppers, cream cheese, Mexican crema, heavy cream, chicken bouillon, baby spinach, and cilantro, along with the cooked onion and garlic. You may need to do this in batches. Blend until fully smooth. If needed, add some of the cooking water from the spaghetti to help thin it.

4   To the same pan, set over medium heat, add the butter.

5   Once melted, add the blended sauce and the cooked spaghetti. Mix until well combined.

6   Taste the sauce and season with salt and pepper as needed.

7   Plate the green spaghetti with crumbled queso fresco. Serve as a side with your favorite protein or main dish.

2 tablespoons unsalted
  butter
1 tablespoon extra-virgin
  olive oil
1½ cups corn, fresh or
  canned
1 jalapeño, finely chopped
4 garlic cloves, grated
1 teaspoon onion salt
1 teaspoon kosher salt, plus
  more for pasta water

1 teaspoon black pepper
1 package cheese-filled
  ravioli, fresh or frozen
1 cup heavy cream
1 cup Mexican crema

for garnish:
Crumbled cotija cheese
Chopped cilantro
Zest and juice of 1 lime
Chile-lime seasoning

street corn ravioli

serves: **4**
prep time: **5 minutes**
cook time: **35 minutes**
total time: **40 minutes**

I first had a version of something like this at a restaurant in Vegas—that dish was good, but not amazing. I immediately knew I could make a much better version at home. So here is my rendition of a street corn elote made into a sauce for ravioli. We're using store-bought ravioli here because it's a time-saver, and the star of this dish is really the sauce. This recipe is completely vegetarian but you can certainly cook some chicken to serve alongside the ravioli, or even add shredded rotisserie chicken into the creamy elote sauce.

1 Bring a large pot of water to a boil.

2 Set a large sauté pan over medium heat. Add the butter and olive oil.

3 Once the butter is melted, add in the corn, jalapeño, and garlic. Mix everything around and cook for 6 to 8 minutes.

4 Add the spices and cook for another 2 minutes.

5 Once the water for the ravioli is boiling, add salt and the ravioli and cook according to the package instructions.

6 To the pan with the corn, add the heavy cream and the Mexican crema. Mix to combine with the corn. Reduce the heat to low and simmer for 8 to 10 minutes.

7 Drain the ravioli, reserving some of the pasta water. Add the ravioli to the sauce and mix around to combine.

8 If the sauce looks too thick, add ¼ cup of pasta water to help thin the sauce. Let it simmer for 4 to 5 more minutes and turn off the heat.

9 To serve, garnish with lots of crumbled cotija cheese, cilantro, lime zest and juice, and a sprinkling of chile lime seasoning.

1 pound spaghetti
10 ounces (280g) Mexican chorizo
1 pound (450g) ground beef
1 small white onion, diced
2 garlic cloves, finely minced or grated
1 teaspoon paprika
1 teaspoon black pepper
1 teaspoon kosher salt
½ teaspoon crushed red pepper flakes
2× 24 ounce (680g) jars marinara
3 cups shredded Muenster cheese

chori-queso baked spaghetti

serves: 4 to 6, with leftovers
prep time: 5 minutes
cook time: 1 hour
total time: 1 hour 20 minutes (including resting time)

This is my take on my mom's spaghetti with ground beef, but I take the extra step of baking it with cheese and chorizo on top. The addition of the chorizo and Muenster cheese combined with the spaghetti makes for an incredibly cozy dish. Everyone loves a good, cheesy spaghetti and the flavor bomb that is chorizo is just the cherry on top.

1   Bring a large pot of water to a boil. Once boiling, add in the spaghetti and cook according to the package instructions.

2   In a large sauté pan over medium-high heat, add the chorizo. Break it down into smaller pieces and cook for 6 to 8 minutes. Remove from the pan and set aside. If your chorizo released a lot of fat, remove all but 1 tablespoon from the pan.

3   In the same pan, add the ground beef and break it into smaller pieces. Cook for 4 to 5 minutes.

4   Add the onion and garlic and cook, stirring frequently, for 4 minutes or until the onion begins to soften.

5   Add in the spices and cook for 2 more minutes.

6   Reduce heat to medium-low and add in the marinara. Mix to combine. Let simmer for 6 to 8 minutes. Taste the meat sauce and adjust any seasonings as needed.

7   Preheat the oven to 350° (180°).

8   In a large mixing bowl, add the sauce and spaghetti and mix until well combined. If your pot is large enough you can mix it in there instead.

9   Using a 9 x 13 inch (22 x 33 cm) baking dish, layer half of the spaghetti, then sprinkle over 1 cup of the shredded cheese and half of the chorizo. Layer the rest of the spaghetti and finish it off with the remaining shredded cheese and the rest of the chorizo.

10 Cover with foil and bake the spaghetti for 12 to 15 minutes. Remove the foil and bake for an additional 5 to 6 minutes, or until the cheese is golden brown and bubbly.

11 Let rest for 10 to 15 minutes before serving (to save your beautiful taste buds).

for the sauce:
6 poblano peppers, roasted, peeled, and seeds removed (see page 16)
½ large white onion
4 garlic cloves
1½ cups Mexican crema
1x 8 ounce (226g) block cream cheese
1 cup chicken broth
6 ounces (170g) baby spinach
1 teaspoon kosher salt
1 teaspoon black pepper

for the lasagna:
2 tablespoons extra-virgin olive oil
1 pound (450g) ground turkey or ground chicken
½ large white onion, finely chopped
1 jalapeño, finely chopped

1 tablespoon chicken bouillon
1 teaspoon ground cumin
1 teaspoon dried Mexican oregano
1 teaspoon kosher salt
1 teaspoon black pepper
2 calabacitas, roughly chopped
1 bunch cilantro, chopped, plus more for garnish
1 pound (453g) requeson or ricotta cheese
1 pound (453g) Muenster cheese, in slices or shredded
1 pound (453g) no-boil lasagna noodles
Mexican crema, for serving

special equipment
Blender

mexican lasagna

serves: **4 to 6**
prep time: **15 minutes**
cook time: **1 hour 15 minutes**
total time: **1 hour 30 minutes**

In Mexico we have pastel azteca, which is essentially a Mexican lasagna made of layered tortillas with a chicken and veggie filling and a creamy green sauce. Here, I'm using the traditional ingredients you'd use for the sauce and filling, but instead of using tortillas we are using lasagna noodles. The result is perfectly filling, creamy, and cheesy—it's sure to be a new family favorite!

I use no-boil noodles for this, but you can use whichever type you prefer.

1   To make the sauce, add all the ingredients to a blender. Blend until smooth.

2   Set a large sauté pan over medium-high heat and add the olive oil. Once hot, add the ground turkey or chicken and break it into smaller pieces. Cook for 4 to 5 minutes.

3   Add the onion, jalapeño, and all the spices. Stir and cook for 4 more minutes.

4   Add the calabacitas and chopped cilantro, and cook for 5 to 6 more minutes. Turn off the heat.

5   Preheat the oven to 375° (190°).

6   Start assembling the lasagna in a rectangular 9 x 13 inch (22 x 33 cm) baking dish.

7   To form the layers, start by pouring about ½ cup of the sauce on the bottom. Next, add an even layer of the lasagna noodles.

8   Sprinkle over about ⅓ of the ground turkey mixture over the lasagna. Break up pieces of the requeson over the meat mixture, sprinkle an even layer of Muenster cheese, then pour over more of the green sauce. Continue assembling the lasagna in that order until you've used up all the ingredients. Making sure the top layer is sauce and cheese.

9   Cover with foil and bake for 30 minutes. Uncover and bake for another 5 to 10 minutes or until perfectly golden brown on top.

10 Once baked, let the lasagna rest for 15 to 20 minutes.

11 Cut into squares and top each slice with a drizzle of Mexican crema and a sprinkling of cilantro.

for the chiles:
8 poblano peppers
1 pound (450g) Muenster
cheese or queso panela,
sliced into planks
1 batch Picadillo (see page
90)
½ cup all-purpose flour

for the batter:
8 eggs, at room
temperature
Oil, for frying

special equipment
Electric hand mixer or stand
mixer, fitted with the
whisk attachment

chiles rellenos

serves: 4 to 6
prep time: 40 minutes
cook time: 50 minutes
total time: 1 hour 30 minutes

This was my absolute favorite thing to have for dinner growing up. I think I loved them even more because my mom wouldn't make them often—they're a bit time-consuming and not the quickest family meal for a typical weeknight. Now don't let that deter you from making them—just because they're time-consuming doesn't mean they're difficult to make. All the steps are simple, there are just quite a few of them. My favorite way to have them is with cheese, but you can use a combination of cheese and picadillo as a filling (see page 90).

make it into... *a carne asada burrito, or a torta. Slather a large flour tortilla with Refried Beans (see page 29) then top with a Chile relleno, warmed through and diced carne asada, chopped lettuce, and diced tomato; wrap it up and enjoy.*

Many times you will see chiles rellenos simmered in a tomato-based, mildly spicy sauce. I skip this step as I find it makes the perfectly crispy chile relleno soft. Instead we simply serve our favorite salsa on the side and top as we please.

1 Start by preparing the peppers. Roast them using whichever method you prefer (see page 16). Once roasted, peel off the skins, carefully make a slit down the length of the peppers (be careful not to cut them all the way through), and scoop out the seeds.

2 For the filling use all cheese, all picadillo, or a mixture of both inside each pepper.

3 To stuff the peppers, add 2 pieces of cheese if only stuffing with cheese; or 1 piece of cheese and a spoonful of picadillo, about ¼ cup; or about ½ cup of picadillo if only filling with that.

4 Coat the stuffed chiles with flour and lay them on a baking sheet. Place in the freezer for 20 to 30 minutes. This will firm up the peppers, make it easier to fry them and eliminates the need to use toothpicks.

5 When ready to fry, start preparing the egg batter.

6 Separate the egg whites from the egg yolks, being extra careful to avoid breaking the yolks as that'll make beating up the egg whites more difficult.

7 Add the egg whites to your mixing bowl and whisk them for about 4 to 6 minutes, starting slowly and increasing speed as you go, or until they more than doubled in size becoming a thick, fluffy batter.

8 One at a time, beat the egg yolks into the egg whites until fully combined. The batter will now be a pale yellow.

9 Add 1 inch (2½ cm) of oil to a wide, shallow sauté pan. Set over medium heat.

10 Working quickly as the egg batter will deflate the longer it sits, start frying the peppers. One at a time, dip them into the egg batter, making sure to fully coat. Carefully lay each pepper in the hot frying oil, cooking 2 to 3 at a time depending on how many comfortably fit in your pan. Using a big spoon, carefully and slowly spoon some of the hot oil over the top of the chiles to start setting the egg batter.

11 Fry on the first side for about 2 minutes, flip over, and fry another 2 minutes or until perfectly golden brown all over.

12 Place the cooked chiles on a paper towel–lined tray to soak up excess oil.

13 Continue frying all chiles using the same method.

14 Serve the chiles with your favorite sides or on tortillas as a taco.

This is the perfect recipe to make with company; the more help you have the smoother the process will be. And, if it's your first time making them, fry one pepper at a time, to start.

The general rule is to use 1 egg for every chile relleno you want to make.

If needed, close the peppers with toothpicks. You can fry with them in, just remember to take them out before eating.

weeknight dinners **143**

2 to 3 boneless skinless
 chicken breasts, diced
1 tablespoon extra-virgin
 olive oil
1 small white onion, diced
1 jalapeño, finely diced
1 teaspoon garlic powder
1 teaspoon kosher salt
1 teaspoon black pepper
1 teaspoon paprika
2 cups canned or jarred
 artichoke hearts, chopped

10 ounces (283g) baby
 spinach
4 to 6 flour tortillas or 8
 corn tortillas (for
 homemade see pages 23
 and 24 or store-bought)
Shredded Chihuahua
 cheese, (as much as you'd
 like, it's a quesadilla,
 after all)
Salsa of choice, for serving
Lime wedges, for serving

spinach artichoke quesadillas

serves: 4
prep time: 5 minutes
cook time: 25 minutes
total time: 30 minutes

We all love a good spinach and artichoke dip with too many tortilla chips. Say hello to the quesadilla version of the iconic app—and with this version, you won't feel guilty about eating it with 20 tortillas' worth of chips (you'll just be eating 1 or 2). It's easy, simple, and ready in about 30 minutes—and will certainly join your rotation of weekly dinners.

1   To a large sauté pan set over medium-high heat, add the extra-virgin olive oil.

2   Once hot, add the chicken, onion, and jalapeño. Mix everything and cook for 6 to 8 minutes or until the onion begins to soften.

3   Add the seasonings, mix to combine, and cook for 3 to 4 more minutes.

4   Add the chopped artichokes and spinach, cover with a lid, and cook for 2 minutes.

5   Uncover the pan, mix everything around, and cook for 3 to 4 more minutes.

6   Taste the filling and adjust the seasonings as needed.

7   To assemble the quesadilla, set a comal over medium heat.

8   Add one flour tortilla to the pan and sprinkle one half with cheese (at least ¼ cup). Add a couple spoonfuls of the filling, sprinkle more cheese on top, and fold the other half of the flour tortilla over. If using corn tortillas, use two of them stacked with the fillings in between rather than folding.

9   Cook the quesadilla for 1 to 2 minutes per side, or until the cheese is perfectly melted. .

10 Repeat the process with all the tortillas and filling.

11 Slice up the quesadillas, serve as is, or finish them off with salsa and a fresh squeeze of lime juice.

for the enchilada sauce:
25 dried guajillo peppers, stems and seeds removed
10 dried chiles de árbol, see Note
1 large white onion, quartered
8 garlic cloves
1 tablespoon kosher salt
1 teaspoon dried Mexican oregano
1 teaspoon ground cumin

for assembly:
20 to 25 corn tortillas (for homemade see pages 23 and 24 or store-bought)
Avocado oil, for frying
2 cups crumbled queso fresco
1 small white onion, finely diced
1 bunch cilantro, finely chopped
Mexican crema

special equipment
Blender

enchiladas rojas

makes: 20 to 25 enchiladas and about 6½ cups enchilada sauce
serves: 4
prep time: 10 minutes
cook time: 45 minutes
total time: 55 minutes

If you're a fan of enchiladas rojas, chances are you've only really had Tex-Mex enchiladas. These are more of the traditional enchiladas rojas you find in Mexico. They're simple to make, vegetarian (but you can add shredded chicken if you'd like), and downright delicious. "Enchilada" is what someone would say when they're eating something and it's too spicy (*"ando bien enchilada(o)"* aka *"my mouth is on fire"*) so these are on the spicier side, but read the Note if you want to tone down the spice. This recipe makes a lot of sauce because you can so easily freeze the extra for use in other recipes in this book. .

If you want to add more protein to these, mix some shredded chicken into the queso fresco mixture.

If you want to make these with no spice, completely leave out the chiles de árbol.

If you want it somewhat spicy, use between 2 to 5 chiles de árbol instead of 10.

1 Add the guajillo and árbol chiles to a large saucepot with enough water to cover and submerge the peppers, about 8 cups.

2 Bring the water to a boil. Once boiling, add the onion and garlic, turn off the heat, cover with a lid, and allow the contents to cool completely. The carryover heat from the water will soften the onion and garlic.

3 Once the peppers have cooled, add them to a blender along with the onion, garlic, salt, oregano, ground cumin, and 3 cups of the chile-soaking water. Blend until smooth. If it seems too thick, add more chile water as needed.

4 If desired, you can pour the enchilada sauce through a fine mesh strainer into a saucepan to remove any large stray pieces of chiles; I find that using a high-powered blender eliminates the need to do this.

5 Set a saucepan over medium-low heat to warm up the enchilada sauce.

6 To start assembling the enchiladas, mix the crumbled queso fresco with the finely diced onion and the cilantro. Mix well to combine.

7 Set a large frying pan over medium-high heat and add ¼ cup avocado oil.

8 One at a time, fry the corn tortillas for about 20 to 30 seconds per side (you want them to become slightly crispy but still be pliable). Continue with all the tortillas, adding more oil as needed.

9 Once all the tortillas are fried, start assembling the enchiladas: pass each fried tortilla through the hot enchilada sauce, place it on a plate, add about 2 to 3 tablespoons of the queso fresco mixture, and roll it up. Continue with all tortillas and filling.

10 Serve 4 to 5 enchiladas per person—drizzle each plate with Mexican crema and a sprinkling of more of the queso fresco mixture.

1 pound (450g) ground beef
1 large white onion, chopped
4 garlic cloves, grated
1 teaspoon kosher salt
1 teaspoon black pepper
1 teaspoon ground cumin
1 tablespoon paprika
1 tablespoon tomato chicken bouillon
5 Roma tomatoes

2½ cups Enchilada Sauce (see page 147)
20 corn tortillas
Avocado oil, for frying
4 cups shredded cheddar

for serving:
Mexican crema
Chopped cilantro
Rice (see page 26)
Beans (see page 29)

tex-mex enchiladas

serves: **4 to 6**
prep time: **5 minutes**
cook time: **45 minutes**
total time: **50 minutes**

I love me some traditional enchiladas, but I also LOVE me some Tex-Mex enchiladas. They're saucy and cheesy, what's not to love?!

They have a bad reputation for some reason, but there is a time and place for them, and when that time comes, they always hit the spot.

1 To a large sauté pan set over medium heat, add the ground beef and break it down with a wooden spoon. Cook for 5 minutes.

2 Add the onion and garlic and stir to combine, cook for 4 to 5 more minutes.

3 Stir in the spices and cook for 5 more minutes.

4 Add the enchilada sauce to a blender with the tomatoes and blend until combined.

5 Pour 1 cup of the blended enchilada sauce into the pan with the ground beef and mix to combine. Pour the rest into a separate pan set over low heat to keep warm.

6 To the blender add in ½ cup of water. Swish it around to get all the sauce out and add it to the pan with the beef.

7 Reduce heat to low and simmer while frying the corn tortillas.

8 To a frying pan set over medium heat, add ¼ cup avocado oil. One at a time, fry the tortillas for about 20 to 30 seconds per side. Add more oil as needed until all tortillas are fried.

9 Preheat the oven to 350°F (180°C).

10 To assemble, fill each tortilla with ¼ cup of the meat filling and 1 to 2 tablespoons of the shredded cheese. Roll them up and place them in a single layer in the baking dish. Continue with all tortillas and filling. You will still have some of the saucy meat filling and cheese left over—this will go on top.

11 Pour the remaining enchilada sauce over the layer of rolled enchiladas, then top with the remaining meat filling and shredded cheese.

12 Cover the baking dish with foil and bake for 15 minutes. Remove the foil and bake for 5 to 6 more minutes.

13 Finish off the baked enchiladas with Mexican crema and chopped cilantro.

14 Serve with a side of rice and beans.

for the sauce:
1 cup mayonnaise
2 to 3 tablespoons dill
  pickle relish
2 tablespoons ketchup
1 tablespoon yellow
  mustard
1 tablespoon white vinegar
1 teaspoon paprika
1 teaspoon onion powder
1 teaspoon garlic powder
1 teaspoon kosher salt
1 teaspoon black pepper
¼ teaspoon cayenne
  pepper

for the flautas:
1 tablespoon avocado oil,
  plus more for frying

1 pound (450g) ground beef
1 small white onion,
  chopped
1 tablespoon paprika
1 tablespoon tomato
  bouillon
1 teaspoon onion powder
1 teaspoon garlic powder
1 teaspoon kosher salt
1 teaspoon black pepper
½ teaspoon cayenne
  pepper
1× 14.5 ounce (411g) can
  fire-roasted diced
  tomatoes
12 to 16 corn tortillas
6 to 12 slices of American
  cheese
Shredded iceberg lettuce
Diced tomatoes

cheeseburger flautas

serves: 4
prep time: **10 minutes**
cook time: **45 minutes**
total time: **55 minutes**

One of the recipes in my usual rotation is flautas and one of my go-to fast food meals is a cheeseburger. You might think the idea of combining the two is crazy, but let me tell you something—these flautas are delicious. Truly one of my wildest creations ever, and I hope you try it too because the kids in your life will be obsessed.

Make these double cheeseburger flautas by topping off the freshly fried flautas with half a slice of American cheese immediately after they've been fried; the carryover heat will melt the cheese.

To make these in the air fryer, spray the flautas with oil and cook at 350°F (180°C) for 12 to 15 minutes, flipping halfway through.

1 To make the sauce, add all the ingredients to a bowl and mix to combine. Taste and adjust seasonings as needed. Refrigerate until ready to use.

2 To make the filling, add the oil to a large sauté pan set over medium heat.

3 Once hot, add the ground beef and start breaking it into smaller pieces. Cook for about 5 minutes.

4 Add the onion and spices, stir, and cook for 5 more minutes.

5 Add the diced tomatoes, stir, and cook for 6 more minutes, stirring frequently. Set the filling aside.

6 Using a slightly damp dish towel or paper towels, wrap the stack of corn tortillas and steam in the microwave for 45 to 60 seconds. Immediately separate the tortillas after microwaving to keep them from sticking together.

7 Assemble the flautas by laying half a piece of American cheese on the tortilla and roughly ¼ cup of filling. Roll it up as tightly as possible and set it aside seam-side down. Continue filling and rolling the flautas until you have used up all the filling.

8 Set a large frying pan over medium-high heat and add enough oil to cover the bottom of the pan.

9 Once hot, working in batches, place the flautas in a single layer in the pan with the seam side facing down. Fry the flautas for 1 to 2 minutes on the first side, until slightly golden. Flip over and fry for another 1 to 2 minutes. When ready, place them on a paper towel–lined plate to soak up any excess oil. Continue frying the rest of the flautas, adding more oil if needed.

10 To serve the flautas, plate as many as you'd like and top them with shredded lettuce, diced tomatoes, and the sauce.

2 pounds (907g) thinly
   sliced steak, about ¼ inch
   (½ cm) thick
1 tablespoon Lawry's
   Seasoned Salt
1 cup all-purpose flour
2 tablespoons paprika
1 teaspoon garlic powder
1 teaspoon onion salt
1 teaspoon kosher salt
1 teaspoon black pepper

4 eggs
1 cup whole milk, or any
   milk of your choosing
2 cups breadcrumbs
Oil, for frying

for serving:
Rice of your choice (see
   page 26)
Beans of your choice (see
   pages 28 and 29)
Side salad

milanesa de res

serves: 4
prep time: **15 minutes**
cook time: **45 minutes**
total time: **1 hour**

Milanesa is another one of the few things I didn't grow up eating simply because my mom never really made it. I think she didn't make it because of the breading and frying process, which can be messy (but so worth it!). Enjoy these with a side salad and some rice, or make a torta with it.

make it into... *a torta, serve the hot and crispy milanesa stuffed into a bolillo or telera with a slather of Refried Beans (see page 29) on the bottom, topped with your favorite cheese, lettuce, tomatoes, pickled jalapeños, salsa of choice, and Mexican crema.*

1   Prepare the steak by poking it all over with a fork on both sides. Season with the seasoned salt all over.

2   Prepare your breading station using 3 disposable aluminum pans (for easy clean up). To the first one, add the flour and the rest of the seasonings, then whisk to combine. To the second one, add the eggs and milk and whisk to combine. To the third pan, add the breadcrumbs.

3   Start breading the steak: first, pass both sides through the flour, making sure it's fully coated. Then pass the floured steak through the egg wash mixture, making sure it's fully coated. Lastly, pass the steak through the breadcrumbs, making sure to pat them in so it's well coated.

4   Place the breaded steaks on a plate and put them in the freezer for 20 to 30 minutes. This will help the breading fully adhere.

5   Get a large frying pan and add enough oil to cover the bottom of the pan with about ½ inch of oil. Set over medium heat.

6   Once the oil is hot, work in batches to fry up the milanesa for 3 to 4 minutes on the first side. Flip over and fry for 2 to 3 more minutes on the second side. They should be perfectly golden brown and crispy.

7   When done cooking, place them on a paper towel–lined baking tray to soak up any excess oil.

8   Continue with the rest of the milanesas, adding more oil if needed.

9   Serve the milanesas with your choice of sides.

2 tablespoons avocado oil
4 Roma tomatoes, quartered
1 small white onion, quartered
5 garlic cloves
½ cup diced chipotle peppers in adobo
1× 8 ounce (226g) block cream cheese, at room temperature
1 cup chicken broth

½ cup Mexican crema or sour cream
1 tablespoon tomato chicken bouillon
2 pounds (907g) chicken breast, cut into cubes
1 teaspoon kosher salt
1 teaspoon black pepper
¼ teaspoon ground cumin
Cooked rice, for serving (my go-to is Rice with Corn, see page 26)

special equipment
Blender

chipotle chicken

serves: 4
prep time: **10 minutes**
cook time: **30 minutes**
total time: **40 minutes**

This is possibly my mom's favorite dish to make, and I'm right there with her. I love this dish so much and I don't make it as often as I should. As Rachael Ray would say, it'll be ready in 30 minutes from start to finish.

1 Set a large sauté pan over medium heat and add 1 tablespoon of the avocado oil.

2 Once hot, add the tomatoes, onion, and garlic. Cook, stirring every minute or so, for 5 to 7 minutes or until the onion has begun to soften.

3 Add the cooked veggies to a blender along with the diced chipotle peppers, cream cheese, chicken broth, tomato bouillon, and Mexican crema. Blend until smooth and set aside

4 To the same sauté pan, add the remaining 1 tablespoon of avocado oil and set over medium-high heat. Once hot, add the diced chicken and cook for about 8 minutes, stirring every minute or so.

5 Add in the spices and cook for 4 more minutes.

6 Add in the blended sauce and stir. Reduce the heat to low and simmer for 10 minutes, stirring every couple of minutes.

7 Serve the chipotle chicken with rice.

5- to 6-pound (2- to 2¾ kg) whole chicken
1 bunch cilantro
1 jalapeño, stem removed
5 green onions, roughly chopped
5 garlic cloves
Zest and juice of 2 limes
1 tablespoon kosher salt
1 tablespoon black pepper
1 teaspoon dried Mexican oregano
½ teaspoon ground cumin
¼ cup olive oil
6 tablespoons unsalted butter, room temperature
1 pound (450g) baby potatoes
Flaky salt

special equipment
Blender
Instant-read thermometer

cilantro lime roast chicken

serves: **4 to 6**
prep time: **20 minutes**
cook time: **2 hours 40 minutes**
total time: **3 hours**

I own a lot of cookbooks and I think one of the most common recipes in every single one is a roasted chicken. I rarely make those recipes, but then I got to thinking, if those roasted chickens tasted great and were juicy, then yeah, I'd make them. The cilantro, lime, and jalapeño in this marinade make this one of the most flavorful chickens you'll ever eat. And if you have leftovers, you're already halfway to making some delicious flautas the next day.

1   Preheat the oven to 350°F (180°C).

2   Pat the chicken dry using paper towels and set it aside at room temperature.

3   To a blender, add the cilantro, jalapeño, green onions, garlic, lime juice, salt, pepper, oregano, cumin, and olive oil, and blend to combine, about 30 seconds.

4   Pour the marinade into a bowl, add the butter, and mix to combine. It will make a slightly thick paste.

5   Rub the cilantro-lime marinade all over the chicken, making sure to get in between the chicken skin and the meat of the chicken. Do this by gently sticking your hands under the skin to lift it up and spreading the marinade under and over the skin.

6   Using a roasting pan, spread the potatoes on the bottom and place the chicken over them. The potatoes will work as the rack while all the juices from the chicken and the marinade will drip onto the potatoes.

7   Cover the pan with aluminum foil and bake for about 2 hours or until an instant-read thermometer reads 165°F (75°C) when inserted into the chicken breast. Cook the chicken covered for the first hour and uncover for the last hour. Once cooked, let rest for 20 to 30 minutes before serving.

8   When ready to serve, cut up the chicken and plate with your favorite sides. Top the potatoes with some flaky salt.

2 pounds (907g) thinly-sliced chicken breasts (see note)
¾ cups all-purpose flour
3 eggs
½ cup milk
2 cups panko breadcrumbs
2 tablespoons paprika
1 teaspoon onion powder
1 teaspoon garlic powder
1 teaspoon kosher salt
1 teaspoon crushed black pepper
Oil, for frying

1 batch Green Spaghetti sauce (see page 135) or Chipotle Chicken sauce (see page 153)
1 pound (450g) spaghetti
2 cups shredded Muenster cheese or mozzarella

for serving:
Mexican crema
Pickled Red Onions (see page 51)
Crumbled queso fresco
Chopped cilantro

mexican chicken parm

serves: **4**
prep time: **5 minutes**
cook time: **45 minutes**
total time: **50 minutes**

I first made a version of this recipe for a partnership I had in promotion of Gordon Ramsay's Next-Level Chef, which was coincidently premiering their second season immediately after the Super Bowl. As if the story couldn't get any crazier, when the episode aired they showed a clip of MY video on the bottom right corner of the TV—still crazy to me—but even crazier that I haven't been on a Gordon Ramsay show! What are y'all waiting for? I'm ready to be humiliated by Mr. Ramsay himself. That being said, lots of my crazy ideas have been born thanks to social media and the need to come up with relevant, out-of-the-box recipes to catch people's attention. This is one of those recipes I probably NEVER would've thought about making six years ago, but damn, is it one of the greatest recipes I have ever made! And now you have to make this, ASAP!

You can be lazy like me and buy already thinly sliced chicken breasts, or you can use whole boneless skinless chicken breasts and slice them up yourself. Pound them to make them even thinner, if desired.

1. Prepare your dredging station using 3 baking trays (I like to use the disposable aluminum pans for easier clean up). To the first one, add the flour and all of the seasonings and whisk to combine. To the second one, add the eggs and milk and whisk to combine. To the third one, add the bread crumbs.

2. Start breading the chicken cutlets: first, pass them through the flour mixture, making sure they're coated all over. Next, pass the floured chicken through the egg wash, making sure they're coated all over. Lastly, pass the chicken through the bread crumbs. Make sure to pat them to get a good coating of bread crumbs. Continue with the rest of the chicken cutlets until all are coated.

3. Set a large frying pan over medium-high heat and add enough oil to cover the bottom with about ½ an inch of oil.

4. Once the oil is hot, start frying the chicken cutlets in batches. Fry the chicken for about 3 minutes on the first side. Once golden brown, flip over and cook on the second side for another 2 to 3 minutes. Once golden brown and crispy all over, set the cooked chicken cutlets on a paper towel–lined baking sheet to soak up any excess oil. Continue frying the rest of the chicken cutlets.

5. Bring a large pot of water to a boil. Once boiling, add about 3 tablespoons of salt and cook the spaghetti according to the package instructions.

6. While the pasta cooks, add the sauce you are using to a large saucepot set over medium heat to warm through.

7. To prepare the chicken cutlets for serving, place them on a baking tray and top each cutlet with about ½ cup of sauce. Then top with ¼ cup of the shredded cheese.

8. Place the loaded chicken cutlets under your oven's broiler for 2 to 4 minutes or until the cheese is golden brown and melted.

9. To serve your chicken parm, toss the cooked spaghetti with the rest of the sauce and plate the spaghetti with some of the sauced cheesy chicken cutlets on top.

10. Garnish each plate with a drizzle of Mexican crema, pickled red onions, and a sprinkling of cilantro.

for the sauce:
6 poblano peppers, roasted, peeled, stems and seeds removed (see page 16)
2 cups chicken broth
1 cup heavy cream
½ cup Mexican crema
½ bunch cilantro
4 garlic cloves
1 teaspoon guajillo chile powder
1 teaspoon ground cumin
1 teaspoon dried oregano
1 tablespoon kosher salt
2 teaspoon black pepper
3 cups shredded rotisserie chicken
4 tablespoons unsalted butter
¼ cup all-purpose flour
2 cups frozen peas

for the filling:
2 tablespoons extra-virgin olive oil
½ large white onion, finely chopped
1 jalapeño, finely chopped
2 carrots, diced
2 celery stalks, diced
1 pound (450g) Yukon Gold potatoes, diced
1 teaspoon garlic powder
1 teaspoon onion salt

for the crust:
1 or 2 homemade or store-bought pie crusts
2 tablespoons unsalted butter, melted

special equipment:
Blender

poblano pot pie

serves: 6
prep time: 20 minutes
cook time: 1 hour
total time: 1 hour 20 minutes

Up until this point I had never had a chicken pot pie. So, of course, the first time I ever made it had to be with a Mexican twist. Add poblano peppers to ANYTHING and it's instantly one of the greatest things you'll ever have. Poblano peppers are so versatile. If you've never had them, don't worry— they're very mild, especially since we'll remove the seeds for this dish. This pot pie will have everyone thinking you spent hours upon hours making it, but it comes together so quickly.

If the crust is getting too dark, cover with foil.

Use 2 pie crusts if you want to do the lattice top. Use 1 pie crust if just laying flat only.

1 Add all ingredients for the sauce to a blender and blend until smooth, about 20 to 30 seconds.

2 To a large sauté pan set over medium heat, add the olive oil. Once hot, add the onion, jalapeño, carrots, and celery. Cook, stirring frequently, for 4 to 5 minutes.

3 Add in the potatoes and cook while stirring for about 6 minutes.

4 Mix in the spices and cook for an additional 4 minutes.

5 Stir in the chicken to combine. Add the butter and mix until fully melted.

6 Add the flour and mix until fully combined.

7 Pour in the blended poblano sauce, reduce the heat to low, and simmer for 10 minutes.

8 Turn off the heat and stir in the peas.

9 Preheat the oven to 350°F (180°C).

10 Pour the filling into a 9 x 13 inch (22 x 33 cm) or 10in (25cm) oval baking dish.

11 Top with the pie crust and brush with the melted butter.

12 Bake for 36 to 40 minutes or until the crust is golden brown.

for the tuna:
1 pound (450g) sushi grade tuna
½ cup soy sauce
1 teaspoon toasted sesame oil
2 tablespoons rice vinegar
1 tablespoon sesame seeds
¼ cup chopped cilantro
1 serrano pepper, thinly sliced
Zest of 1 lime

for the spicy lime mayo:
1 cup kewpie mayo
Juice of 1 lime

1 tablespoon soy sauce
3 tablespoons sriracha, plus more to taste

for assembling/serving:
Cooked rice or mixed greens
1 cup edamame
1 cup shredded cabbage
1 cup diced mango
3 small cucumbers, diced
Pickled Red Onions (see page 51)
Crushed Hot Cheetos (trust me!)
Tajin or chile-lime seasoning, for sprinkling

chile-lime poke bowls

serves: **4 to 6**
prep time: **10 minutes**
cook time: **30 minutes**
total time: **40 minutes**

It's no secret that I love super indulgent heavy foods, who doesn't? But on the days when I want something lighter, this is one of the things I gravitate toward. It's the ultimate "you do you" type of recipe because aside from the marinated tuna, you can add whatever you're in the mood for. It's light, refreshing, and totally filling.

I get my sushi grade tuna from the freezer section of my local asian market. If you have an H-E-B with a sushi counter, you could also ask the workers there for tuna.

1   Cut the tuna into small cubes and add to a mixing bowl.

2   Add the rest of the ingredients for the tuna marinade, mix to combine, and refrigerate for at least 20 minutes.

3   Make the Spicy Lime Mayo by adding the mayo, lime juice, and soy sauce, and sriracha to a bowl and mixing to combine.

4   When ready to assemble, start your poke bowl with a bed of rice, mixed greens, or a mixture of both.

5   Add about ⅓ cup of the marinated tuna, then add whichever toppings you're using.

6   Finish with a drizzle of the Spicy Lime Mayo and enjoy!

soups & salads

creamy enchilada soup 164

chicken tortilla soup 167

caldo de albondigas 168

sopa de fideo 171

pozole rojo 172

green chili 175

mexican-ish greek salad 176

poblano caesar salad 179

for the soup:
2 tablespoons extra-virgin olive oil
1 small white onion, finely chopped
4 garlic cloves, grated
1 teaspoon smoked paprika
1 teaspoon Italian seasoning
1 teaspoon kosher salt
1 teaspoon black pepper
½ teaspoon whole cumin seeds
3 tablespoons diced chipotle peppers in adobo
1 cup Enchilada Sauce (see page 147)
1× 28 ounce (794g) can crushed tomatoes
1× 28 ounce (794g) can whole peeled tomatoes
2 cups chicken broth
1 cup heavy cream
Goat cheese, optional
Mexican crema, for drizzling
Chopped fresh cilantro, for garnish

for the grilled cheese:
8 slices of your favorite bread
12 slices of your favorite melting cheeses (I use a combination of Muenster, cheddar, and mozzarella)
Olive oil, for toasting

creamy enchilada soup
with grilled cheese

serves: 4
prep time: 5 minutes
cook time: 45 minutes
total time: 50 minutes

This is my very Mexican version of a grilled cheese and tomato soup. Here I use my homemade Enchilada Sauce (see page 147), which I encourage you to use as well, but you can also use store-bought enchilada sauce. If you do use the homemade sauce and you made it spicy, the soup will also be spicy, which is why I love it so much.

1 Set a large soup pot or Dutch oven over medium heat and add the extra-virgin olive oil.

2 Once hot, add the onion and garlic. Cook for 4 to 5 minutes or until the onion begins to soften. Add the spices, stir to combine, and cook for 1 minute.

3 Add the chipotle peppers, enchilada sauce, and the can of crushed tomatoes. Stir to combine.

4 Add the whole tomatoes one at a time, crushing each one with your hand before adding. Repeat for the whole can.

5 Add the chicken broth and let the soup simmer for 10 minutes, stirring occasionally.

6 Add the heavy cream and reduce the heat to low. Let simmer while you make the grilled cheeses.

7 Set your comal or large nonstick skillet over medium heat.

8 Assemble the grilled cheeses by adding three slices of cheese to each piece of bread, then top them off with the second piece of bread.

9 Drizzle olive oil on the comal, place each sandwich on it, and drizzle the top with more olive oil.

10 Cook on the first side for about 2 minutes or until golden brown, flip, and cook another 2 to 3 minutes on the second side. Continue flipping every minute or until the cheese is gooey and fully melted.

11 Serve the soup in bowls. Garnish each bowl of soup with a scoop of goat cheese, a drizzle of Mexican crema, a sprinkling of cilantro, and a grilled cheese on the side to dip into the soup.

- 1 pound (450g) tomatillos, husked and rinsed
- 6 ounces (170g) baby spinach
- 4 garlic cloves
- 1 large white onion
- 4 cups chicken broth
- 2 tablespoons avocado oil
- 1 jalapeño, finely diced
- 1 bell pepper, diced
- 1 poblano pepper, diced
- 1 cup carrots, finely diced
- 1 tablespoon chicken bouillon
- 1 teaspoon cumin
- 1 teaspoon oregano
- 1 teaspoon guajillo chile powder
- 1 teaspoon kosher salt
- 1 teaspoon black pepper
- 2 pounds (907g) boneless, skinless chicken breasts
- 4 calabacitas or 2 zucchini, roughly chopped
- 2 cups corn kernels, canned or frozen

for serving:
Crispy fried tortillas or store-bought crushed tortilla chips
Pickled Red Onions (see page 51)
Limes
Sliced avocado
Crumbled queso fresco
Mexican crema
Chopped fresh cilantro

special equipment
Blender

chicken tortilla soup
(but make it green)

serves: **4 to 6**
prep time: **10 minutes**
cook time: **50 minutes**
total time: **1 hour**

Why are tortilla soups always red? Nearly all chicken tortilla soups are made with a tomato-based broth, chicken, veggies, and toppings that include crispy tortillas. And don't get me wrong, there is nothing wrong with a classic tortilla soup, but for the sake of this book and my brain going into overdrive coming up with new recipes, I landed on this one and was so happy. It just goes to show how much I truly love using poblano peppers and how I'll make any excuse to use them.

1. Add the tomatillos, baby spinach, garlic cloves, half the white onion, and 2 cups of the chicken broth to a blender. Blend until fully combined.

2. To a large soup pot or Dutch oven set over medium heat, add the oil.

3. Once hot, add in the jalapeño, bell pepper, poblano pepper, carrots, and the remaining half of the onion, finely chopped.

4. Add in the spices, mix around, and cook the veggies with the spices for 4 to 5 minutes.

5. Pour in the blended tomatillo mixture, the remaining 2 cups of chicken broth, and 6 cups of water.

6. Gently add in the chicken breasts. Bring to a boil, cover, and reduce the heat to low. Cook until the chicken is done, about 20 to 25 minutes.

7. Remove the chicken from the pot and add in the calabacitas and corn.

8. Shred the chicken and add it back to the pot. Stir everything to combine.

9. Raise heat back to medium and cook for another 10 to 15 minutes or until the calabacitas are cooked through.

10. Taste the soup broth and add any additional seasonings as needed.

11. Serve the soup in bowls with a mountain of crispy tortillas, sliced avocado, crumbled queso fresco, a drizzle of Mexican crema, cilantro, pickled red onions, and a fresh squeeze of lime juice.

- 2 pounds (907g) ground beef
- 1 small white onion, finely chopped
- 1 bunch fresh cilantro, finely chopped
- ¼ cup, plus 2 tablespoons diced chipotle peppers in adobo
- 1 teaspoon guajillo chile powder
- 1 teaspoon ground cumin
- 1 tablespoon kosher salt
- 1 teaspoon black pepper
- ½ cup jasmine rice
- 2 eggs
- 6 garlic cloves
- 1 tablespoon tomato bouillon
- 2 teaspoons dried Mexican oregano
- 4 Roma tomatoes
- 8 cups chicken broth
- 2 carrots, diced
- 1 pound (453g) Yukon gold potatoes, diced
- 3 ears of corn on the cob, cut into 3 pieces
- 3 calabacitas, chopped

for serving:
Cooked rice
Limes wedges
Corn Tortillas (for homemade see page 24 or store-bought)

special equipment
Blender

caldo de albondigas

serves: 6 to 8
prep time: 15 minutes
cook time: 1 hour 15 minutes
total time: 1 hour 30 minutes

Although very popular in the Mexican food world, I never grew up eating albondigas. It's one of the few dishes my mom and the rest of my family just never made. Once I started sharing cooking videos online, albondigas were one of the most requested recipes people wanted me to make. And when I finally made them and shared the video, it immediately blew up and became my most-watched video ever on Instagram. Not only that, it's also the one recipe that people have cooked the most to this day. It's simply that good.

1. To a large mixing bowl add the ground beef, half the onion, half the cilantro, ¼ cup chipotle peppers in adobo, chile powder, cumin, salt, pepper, rice, and eggs. Mix until fully combined.

2. Form the mixture into meatballs about the size of a golf ball; the mix should make about 24 meatballs. Place them on a sheet pan and refrigerate until ready to use.

3. To a blender, add the remaining chopped onion and cilantro, 6 cloves of garlic, tomato bouillon, Mexican oregano, the remaining 2 tablespoons of chipotle peppers, Roma tomatoes, and 4 cups of the chicken broth. Blend until smooth.

4. Add the blended sauce to a large soup pot with the remaining 4 cups of chicken broth and an additional 6 cups of water. Set to medium-high heat and bring to a boil.

5. Once boiling, reduce heat to medium, add the albondigas, and cook for 12 to 15 minutes.

6. Add the diced carrots, potatoes, and corn and cook for 10 more minutes.

7. Add the calabacitas and cook for about 15 to 20 more minutes. Remove from heat.

8. Taste the broth and season with more salt and pepper, if needed.

9. Serve the albondigas 2 to 3 per bowl with some of the broth, veggies, and a scoop of rice.

10. Finish the caldo with a fresh squeeze of lime juice and tortillas for dipping in the broth.

4 Roma tomatoes
½ small white onion
1 jalapeño, stem removed
4 garlic cloves
1 tablespoon tomato bouillon
1 teaspoon kosher salt
1 teaspoon black pepper
4 cups chicken broth
2 tablespoons avocado oil

7 ounces (198g) fideo noodles (vermicelli)
½ bunch cilantro

for serving
Tortillas, of choice
Mayonnaise
Lime juice

special equipment
Blender

sopa de fideo

serves: **4**
prep time: **5 minutes**
cook time: **25 minutes**
total time: **30 minutes**

This is the Mexican version of chicken noodle soup. If a comforting hug was food, this would be it. It's a nostalgic soup I love to make because it's shocking how easy it is and reminds me of simpler times when I was younger. If you've never had sopa de fideo, you're in for a treat. My favorite way to enjoy it is with a warmed-up corn tortilla slathered with a bit of mayo and dipped into the sopita.

1 To a blender add the tomatoes, onion, jalapeño, garlic cloves, tomato bouillon, salt, pepper, and chicken broth. Blend until fully combined.

2 To a soup pot set over medium heat, add the oil. Once hot add in the fideo.

3 Stirring frequently to make sure the fideo doesn't burn, cook until well toasted and darkened in color, about 6 minutes.

4 Pour in the broth plus 1 cup of water, raise heat to medium-high, and mix to combine. Once it comes to a boil, reduce heat to low and simmer for 10 minutes.

5 Add in the cilantro and simmer for 5 more minutes. Remove from heat, taste the broth, and adjust any seasonings as needed.

6 Serve in bowls with a fresh squeeze of lime juice.

The jalapeño doesn't make the soup spicy, but if serving to kids, you can completely leave out the jalapeño or remove the seeds.

Add more protein to this soup by serving with the Picadillo (see page 90): simply serve the fideo and top it off with a couple of spoonfuls of warm picadillo.

20 dried guajillo peppers, stems and seeds removed
6 dried ancho peppers, stems and seeds removed
5 dried chiles de árbol, stems removed
6 to 8 pounds (2½ to 3½ kg) boneless pork shoulder, cut into 2- to 3-inch (5 to 7½cm) pieces
1 head of garlic, plus 8 garlic cloves
5 dried bay leaves
1 large white onion
2 tablespoons kosher salt
1 tablespoon black pepper

3 teaspoons dried Mexican oregano
1 teaspoon ground cumin
1× 110 ounce (3 kg) can of Mexican hominy, drained and rinsed

for serving:
Finely chopped onion
Chopped cilantro
Thinly sliced radishes
Shredded cabbage
Lime wedges
Salsa macha

special equipment
Blender

pozole rojo

serves: **10 to 12**
prep time: **20 minutes**
cook time: **2 hours 40 minutes**
total time: **3 hours**

Pozole rojo is a classic Mexican soup served for holidays and special occasions. Maybe because it's so easy to make—just dump everything into a pot, stir every now and then, and boom! Serve this with toppings like shredded cabbage, thinly sliced radishes, fresh lime juice, and salsa macha to make every bowl your own.

1 To a large saucepan set over high heat, add the dried chiles and enough water to cover them. Let it come to a boil. Once boiling, turn off the heat and let cool down.

2 To a large soup pot, add 20 to 24 cups of water. Add the onion, bay leaves, and head of garlic. Set over high heat and let it come to a boil (about 20 minutes).

3 Once boiling, add the pork, salt, pepper, 2 teaspoons of oregano, and cumin.

4 Reduce the heat to medium and cook for 30 minutes.

5 To a blender, add the rehydrated chiles, 2 cups of the soaking water, the onion from the pork, the cloves of garlic, and the remaining teaspoon of oregano. Blend until smooth.

6 Pour the blended chiles into the pot with the pork. Cover and cook on medium heat for an additional hour.

7 Add in the drained hominy and cook for 30 more minutes, or until the pork is fully cooked through and easily shreddable.

8 When the pork is ready, remove from the pot, shred, and break up into smaller pieces. Remove the head of garlic and the bay leaves and add the pork back into the pot.

9 Serve up the pozole in bowls and garnish with your toppings of choice.

for the chili:
1 tablespoon avocado oil
1 pound (450g) ground pork
or ground chicken
1 large white onion, diced
1 jalapeño, diced
4 cloves garlic, grated
1 teaspoon cumin
1 teaspoon Mexican
oregano
1 tablespoon kosher salt
2 teaspoons black pepper
2 calabacitas or 1 zucchini,
diced
4 poblano peppers, roasted,
peeled, and seeds
removed (see page 16)
4 tomatillos, husks removed
and rinsed
10 ounces (280g) baby
spinach

4 cups veggie or chicken
broth
1× 15.2 ounce (432g) can
white or pinto beans (1
cup)
1× 25 ounce (700g) can
hominy, drained and
rinsed

for serving:
Tortilla chips or Fritos
Mexican crema
Lime wedges
Pickled Red Onions (see
page 51)
Crumbled queso fresco or
shredded cheese of
choice
Shredded cabbage
Sliced radishes

special equipment
Blender

green chili

serves: **4 to 6**
prep time: **10 minutes**
cook time: **1 hour**
total time: **1 hour 10 minutes**

This chili is a play on American red chili made with
tons of ground beef, tomatoes, and beans. It's my
Mexican version made with ground pork and all the
Mexican basics, like roasted poblano peppers,
tomatillos, jalapeños, cumin, and oregano. And of
course, you have to serve it the way you would an
American Frito pie, with tons of toppings like
Mexican crema, Frito chips (or tortilla chips), and
whatever else you're in the mood for.

1 In a large Dutch oven or heavy bottom pot set over
medium heat, heat the oil.

2 Once hot, add the ground pork and break into smaller
pieces with a wooden spoon. Cook for about 5
minutes.

3 Stir in the onion, garlic, and jalapeño, and cook for 3 to
4 minutes.

4 Stir in the spices and cook for 3 to 4 more minutes.

5 Add in the calabacitas and mix to combine.

6 To a blender, add the roasted poblano peppers,
tomatillos, spinach, and 2 cups of the broth. Blend until
fully combined, about 30 seconds.

7 Pour the sauce into the pot with the ground pork and
add the remaining 2 cups of broth.

8 Add the beans and the hominy and mix well to
combine.

9 Raise the heat to high and bring to a boil, stirring to
make sure nothing burns or sticks to the pot.

10 Once boiling, reduce heat to low and let simmer for 20
minutes, stirring every 5 minutes or so.

11 Taste the chili and adjust any seasonings if needed.

12 Serve in bowls with your desired toppings.

for the feta marinade:
1 bunch cilantro
1 garlic clove
¼ small white onion
1 cup extra-virgin olive oil
¼ cup red wine vinegar
Zest and juice of 1 lime
1 teaspoon dried Mexican
   oregano
½ teaspoon whole cumin
   seed
1 jalapeño, roughly
   chopped

1 teaspoon kosher salt
1 teaspoon black pepper

for the salad:
1 to 2 pounds (450 to 900g)
   feta, in blocks (see note)
4 cups cherry tomatoes,
   halved
1 English cucumber, diced
½ red onion, thinly sliced
Extra-virgin olive oil, for
   drizzling

special equipment
Blender

mexican-ish greek salad

serves: **4 to 6**
prep time: **5 minutes**
cook time: **25 minutes**
total time: **30 minutes (plus marinating time)**

I love Greek salads. I have ever since college when
the go-to place to order food on weekends had the
best Greek salad ever. I've been eating them ever
since and I randomly had the idea to marinate the
feta in a cilantro-lime marinade. I'm so glad I did it
because I don't think I'll ever make a Greek salad
any other way. Even my friends who usually don't
like feta cheese love this salad.

1   Add all ingredients for the feta marinade to your
    blender and blend until combined, 20 to 30 seconds.

2   To a container that can fit all the feta, pour some of the
    marinade in the bottom. Add the feta cheese and pour
    over the remaining marinade, making sure it's all well
    coated. Marinate for at least 2 hours or up to overnight.

3   When ready to assemble, take one pound of the
    marinated feta and cut it up into bite-sized cubes.

4   To a large bowl or serving tray, scatter the cubed feta,
    cherry tomatoes, cucumber, and onion.

5   Spoon over a bit more of the feta marinade and finish
    with a drizzle of olive oil.

6   Serve as a side with your favorite dishes.

*This makes more marinated feta than you need for the
recipe, but the marinated feta keeps well in the fridge for
about 2 weeks. It's great for snacking as is, or you can enjoy
it with crackers or make a second round of the salad.*

for the dressing:
1 cup mayonnaise
4 poblano peppers, prepped and roasted (see page 16)
6 anchovies or 2 tablespoons anchovy paste
1 cup freshly grated Parmesan or ¾ cup pre-grated Parmesan
Juice of 1 lemon
2 garlic cloves, grated
1 tablespoon freshly cracked black pepper

for the chicken:
3 to 4 boneless skinless chicken breasts
2 teaspoons kosher salt

2 teaspoons black pepper
2 teaspoons paprika
1 teaspoon garlic powder
1 teaspoon onion salt
1 teaspoon lemon pepper
¼ teaspoon ground cumin
2 tablespoons avocado oil

for the salad:
2 to 3 heads of romaine lettuce, washed and roughly chopped
1 cup croutons
½ cup freshly grated Parmesan
Juice of 1 lemon

special equipment
Immersion blender

poblano caesar salad

serves: **4**
prep time: **10 minutes**
cook time: **45 minutes**
total time: **55 minutes**

Caesar salads have always been my favorite salad, and when I discovered it originated in Mexico, I fell even more in love with them. There's absolutely nothing wrong with the OG Caesar salad, but adding roasted poblanos to the dressing really adds that much-needed mild pepper taste—plus, it gives the dressing an irresistible color. Use store-bought croutons or make it even better by crisping up torn pieces of sourdough bread with lots of olive oil in your air fryer.

1 Make the salad dressing by adding all the ingredients to a large mason jar. Using an immersion blender, mix the dressing until the peppers are fully blended. Taste it and adjust any seasonings, if needed. Refrigerate until ready to assemble.

2 For the chicken, mix the seasonings and season the chicken breasts all over.

3 To a large sauté pan set over medium-high heat, add the oil. Once hot, add the chicken breasts and cook for 4 minutes on the first side. Flip the chicken, cover the pan with a lid, reduce the heat to low, and cook for 12 more minutes. After 12 minutes turn off the heat and leave the chicken covered while you start assembling the salad. The chicken will continue cooking in the covered pan while staying warm for serving.

4 Add the salad to a large mixing bowl and add ½ cup of the dressing. Mix to combine.

5 Remove the chicken from the pan and slice it up.

6 For my favorite assembly, using a sheet pan, add the dressed greens as the first layer. Spread the sliced chicken on top of the greens and top with the croutons, freshly grated parm, and a fresh squeeze of lemon juice. Serve with more Caesar dressing on the side.

make it into..._a caesar salad wrap. Add the dressed romaine lettuce with some of the chicken and croutons to a large flour tortilla and wrap it up. Serve with extra dressing on the side for dipping._

small plates & party food

birria...184

valentina wings.............................188

mango chamoy wings...............191

sweet & spicy macha wings.....192

elotes/esquites...........................197

elote nachos 198

elote foccacia..............................201

jalapeño popper fritters............202

honey chipotle chicken &
    waffles....................................205

papas enchiladas.......................206

chorizo poutine 209

ribeye aguachile........................210

mole...212

birria

serves: **6 with leftovers**
prep time: **15 minutes**
cook time: **4 hours**
total time: **4 hours 15 minutes**

Birria is everywhere these days, and for a good reason—it's absolutely delicious! And you can make so much more with it than just tacos. I love making it in big batches even though I live alone. That's because it's so easy to store in the freezer for 4 to 6 months. I divide the leftovers into deli containers (you can also use zip-top bags)—just make sure to label what it is and when you made it. When you're ready to use it you don't even need to defrost it. I add it to a large enough pot with about 1 cup of water, set it over medium heat and you'll have birria in about 10 minutes.

6 pounds (2¾ kg) beef chuck roast, cut into 4-inch (10 cm) cubes
7 teaspoons salt
4 teaspoons black pepper
1 tablespoon avocado oil
20 dried guajillo peppers, stems and seeds removed
5 dried ancho peppers, stems and seeds removed
5 chiles de árbol, stems removed (optional)
1 onion, quartered
10 garlic cloves
5 dried bay leaves
2-inch (5 cm) piece ginger, peeled
1 teaspoon dried oregano
1 teaspoon whole cumin seeds
3 whole cloves
2 Roma tomatoes
2 tablespoons white vinegar

special equipment
Blender

1   Season the chuck roast pieces with salt and pepper.

2   Set a large Dutch oven or heavy-bottomed pot over medium heat and add the oil.

3   In batches, sear the chuck roast on each side for 1 minute or until a nice crust has formed.

4   Once all the chuck has been seared add it all back to the pot along with the dried peppers.

5   Add in the onion, bay leaves, garlic cloves, ginger, and 8 cups of water. Bring the pot to a boil, reduce heat to low, and simmer, covered, for 2 hours.

6   After 2 hours remove the chiles, garlic, and onions from the pot and add them to a blender.

7   Add the tomatoes, oregano, cumin seeds, garlic, white vinegar, and 2 cups of the cooking liquid from the beef. Blend until fully combined.

8   Add the pureed peppers back to the pot with the chuck and stir to combine. Cover with a lid and simmer for 1 more hour or until the beef is tender and easily shreddable.

9   Remove the birria from the pot and shred it with two forks.

10 Remove the ginger and bay leaves from the pot.

11 Add the shredded birria back to the pot and mix to combine.

12 Serve the birria as tacos with small bowls of the comsommé on the side for dipping.

Birria has become so popular in recent years, and you can use it for so much more than just quesabirria tacos. Here are some of my favorite applications. None of these recipes have set measurements, they are meant to be quick and dirty.

2 large flour tortillas (for homemade see page 23 or store-bought)
Shredded Chihuahua cheese
Birria (see page 184), warmed through
Cilantro, finely chopped
Onion, finely chopped
Salsa macha
guacamole
Lime wedges

1 ball pizza dough, fresh or frozen
Salsa Roja (see page 52)
Birria (see page 184)
Shredded Chihuahua cheese
Finely chopped cilantro
Finely chopped onion
Salsa macha

Crispy tortilla chips
Salsa Roja (see page 52)
Birria (see page 184)
Shredded Chihuahua cheese
Finely chopped cilantro
Finely chopped onion
Mexican crema
Pickled Red Onions (see page 51)
Fried Eggs

mexican pizza

Set a comal over medium heat, add one tortilla, and flip after 30 seconds. Add some shredded cheese, then some birria, then more cheese. Sprinkle some cilantro, onion, and salsa macha over it. Top off with the second tortilla. Cook for 2 minutes, then carefully flip over and cook another 2 minutes or so on the second side. Place onto a cutting board and cut into triangles. Serve with the guacamole, a squeeze of lime, and the warm consommé from the birria for dipping.

american pizza

Preheat the oven to 375°F (190°C). Spray a baking sheet with oil and spread the pizza dough onto the baking sheet. Spread some salsa roja on the bottom of the dough, top it off with some of the birria, and sprinkle all over with shredded Chihuahua cheese. Bake for 15 to 18 minutes, or until the cheese is bubbly and the crust is crispy. Top off the baked pizza with salsa macha, cilantro, and onion, and dip into the warmed consommé.

chilaquiles

In a large frying pan set over medium heat, add about 1 cup of salsa roja and about 1 cup of birria with some of the consommé. Once hot, add in the tortilla chips and mix to combine. Plate the chilaquiles with a sprinkling of shredded cheese, Mexican crema, cilantro, onion, a fried egg, and pickled red onions.

birria matrix

Olive oil, for toasting
Sourdough bread, sliced
Shredded Chihuahua cheese
Birria (see page 184)
Finely chopped cilantro
Finely chopped onion
Salsa macha
Lime wedges

grilled cheese

Set a comal over medium heat, add a light coating of olive oil, and add one slice of sourdough bread. Sprinkle over some shredded cheese and add the birria, cilantro, onion, and another sprinkling of cheese, then place the second piece of bread on top and continue cooking until the cheese has started to melt. Carefully flip over and cook for another 2 to 3 minutes, or until all the cheese has melted and the bread is perfectly crispy. Serve the grilled cheese with a bowl of the warm birria consommé topped with salsa macha and lime wedges.

Oil, for frying
Frozen egg roll wrappers, thawed
Birria (see page 184)
Shredded Chihuahua cheese
Finely chopped cilantro
Finely chopped onion

egg rolls

To a large frying pan set over medium heat, add enough oil to cover the bottom of the pan. Assemble the egg rolls by sprinkling some cheese in the center and topping it off with the birria, cilantro, and onion. Roll it up like a burrito. Fry the egg rolls for 2 to 3 minutes per side or until golden brown and crispy. Serve with warm consommé from the birria for dipping.

for the wings:
3 to 4 pounds (1 to 1¾ kg)
   chicken wings
¼ cup cornstarch
1 tablespoon kosher salt
1 tablespoon black pepper
Cooking oil spray

for the sauce:
4 tablespoons unsalted
   butter
4 garlic cloves, grated
1 cup Valentina hot sauce,
   plus more if desired
½ teaspoon onion powder

for serving:
Chopped cilantro
Ranch or blue cheese
   dressing

valentina wings

serves: **4**
prep time: **5 minutes**
cook time: **35 minutes**
total time: **40 minutes**

One of my all-time favorite store-bought hot sauces is Valentina. They make a mild version and a spicier version, and you can use either for this recipe. You can find it in most grocery stores by the other hot sauces or in the Hispanic section or online in a pinch.

1 Preheat the oven or air fryer to 375°F (190°C).

2 Add the wings to a large mixing bowl along with the cornstarch, kosher salt, and black pepper. Toss to fully coat the wings.

3 Spray the bottom of a baking sheet with oil, lay out the wings in a single layer, and then spray the top with more oil. Use a second baking sheet if needed.

4 Bake or air fry the wings for 22 to 25 minutes, flipping halfway through.

5 While the wings are cooking add the butter to a saucepan set over medium heat.

6 Once the butter is melted add in the garlic and onion powder, stir and cook for 1 minute.

7 Add in the Valentina hot sauce, reduce heat to medium-low and cook for 7 to 10 minutes, stirring every 2 to 3 minutes.

8 Once the wings are ready, add them to a large mixing bowl, and toss them with the sauce.

9 Garnish the wings with cilantro and serve with ranch or blue cheese dressing.

for the wings:
4 pounds (1¾ kg) chicken wings
½ cup cornstarch
1 tablespoon kosher salt
1 tablespoon Chile lime seasoning
1 tablespoon paprika
1 teaspoon onion powder
1 teaspoon garlic powder
1 teaspoon black pepper
Cooking oil spray
Chopped cilantro, for garnish

for the sauce:
3 to 4 dried chiles árbol, stems removed
½ cup chamoy
1 cup honey
2 cups diced mango
½ medium white onion
2 garlic cloves
2 limes, juiced
¼ cup soy sauce
1 teaspoon guajillo chile powder
1 teaspoon cayenne pepper
1 teaspoon Chile lime seasoning
1 teaspoon kosher salt
1 teaspoon black pepper
4 tablespoons unsalted butter

special equipment
Blender

mango chamoy wings

serves: **4**
prep time: **5 minutes**
cook time: **40 minutes**
total time: **45 minutes**

As soon as I knew this book was officially happening, this was the first recipe I developed. Buffalo wings are my favorite food group—I would eat them every single day if I could! A very popular flavor these days is mango habanero, but I didn't want to be basic, so I came up with these. Using Chamoy as the base for this sauce is brilliant—I know you'll agree.

1 Preheat the oven or air fryer to 375°F (190°C).

2 Add the wings to a large bowl along with the cornstarch, salt, Chile lime seasoning, paprika, onion powder, garlic powder, and black pepper. Toss well to make sure all wings are fully coated.

3 Spray the bottom of a baking sheet with oil, lay out the wings in a single, even layer (using more than one cookie sheet, if needed). Once the wings are spread out, spray the tops with oil.

4 Bake or air fry the wings for 25 minutes.

5 To a dry saucepan set over medium heat, add the chiles and pan fry for 30 seconds, then transfer them to the blender.

6 While the wings are cooking, add all ingredients for the sauce, except the butter, to a blender. Blend until smooth.

7 Add the butter to a medium saucepan set over medium heat. Once the butter is melted add the blended sauce and cook, stirring frequently, for 7 to 10 minutes. Reduce the heat to low until the wings are ready.

8 Once the wings are cooked, add them to a large bowl and toss them in the sauce.

9 Plate them up and garnish with cilantro.

for the wings:
3 to 4 pounds (1 to 1¾ kg) chicken wings
⅓ cup cornstarch
1 tablespoon kosher salt
1 tablespoon black pepper
Cooking oil spray

for the sauce:
⅓ cup salsa macha, plus 1 tablespoon of the oil from the jar
4 garlic cloves, grated
½ cup honey
¼ cup soy sauce
Cilantro, for garnish
Crushed peanuts, for garnish

special equipment
Air fryer

sweet & spicy macha wings

serves: **4 to 6**
prep time: **5 minutes**
cook time: **45 minutes**
total time: **50 minutes**

Besides breakfast foods, chicken wings of any kind are my favorite food to eat. I would legit eat them every single day if I could. To me, the ideal chicken wing must be either spicy or sweet. If you've got an air fryer (who doesn't these days?) you can have wings ready in about 30 minutes. The trick is to toss the wings in cornstarch before cooking to make them extra crispy.

1 Pat the chicken wings dry and add them to a large mixing bowl.

2 Add the cornstarch, salt, and pepper. Toss to combine.

3 Set your air fryer to 375°F (190°C).

4 Spray the bottom of your air fryer basket with oil and place the wings in a single layer.

5 Cook the wings for 25 to 30 minutes, flipping halfway through.

6 While the wings cook, prepare the sauce. Set a saucepan over medium heat and add the salsa macha, oil, and garlic.

7 Stir the garlic to combine with the salsa macha and cook for 1 to 2 minutes. Add the honey and soy sauce and stir to combine.

8 Let the sauce cook on medium heat for 4 to 5 minutes, stirring frequently. Then reduce the heat to the lowest setting possible and stir every couple of minutes, or until the wings are ready to be sauced.

9 When the wings are done cooking, add them to a clean mixing bowl. Pour in the sauce and toss to combine.

10 Plate the chicken wings and garnish them with crushed peanuts and cilantro.

If you don't have an air fryer you can cook the wings on a baking sheet in your oven set to 375°F (190°C) for about 40 to 45 minutes, flipping them over halfway through.

Love Story To...
elotes

Growing up in Chicago, the summer sounds of the elotero honking his horn in the near distance was one of my favorite sounds ever. I would immediately go up to my mom and ask for $1.50 (that's how cheap they were back in the day) so I could go get an elote en vaso, aka an esquite, aka corn in a cup. Over time we found our favorite elotero, and we still get elotes from him to this day. Of course, now they're about $4, but still so worth it.

I don't know what it is about elotes that just makes them the greatest snack food OF ALL TIME. I would have them for dinner if I could (and I have). They're the perfect mixture of all ingredients to give you the perfect buttery, cheesy, creamy, tangy, and slightly spicy experience all in one.

The type of elote you end up with will depend greatly on where you are getting it.

The traditional Chicago elotes have yellow corn, mayo, cotija cheese, butter (the fake Parkay variety), and come optionally topped off with spicy chile powder and a fresh squeeze of lime juice.

And the age-old question—what is the difference between esquites and elotes? Well, elotes will be served whole on the cob while esquites will be served in a cup or bowl. In Mexico and in some places in the States, it will include white corn, mayo, crema, cotija cheese, and a spicy, tangy chile sauce (see page 197).

Recently, elotes have risen in popularity in the States—where I live, in McAllen, Texas, there are many places where you can get a delicious elote with crazy, but delicious, toppings.

My go-to place, La Eloteca, gives you the option to pick from mayo, crema, nacho cheese, lime, and cotija cheese. Pick some or all. I pick them all. Then you can opt for additional toppings, like crushed Hot Cheetos, Takis, Ruffles, and even spicy Japanese peanuts. I do Hot Cheetos, Ruffles, and Japanese peanuts. Lastly, you can finish it off with your choice of sauces: the traditional red chile sauce or a habanero, chipotle, jalapeño, or botanera. I typically go for the traditional and either the habanero or chipotle depending on how spicy I'm feeling. And finally, a new one for me, topping the entire bowl with toasted sesame seeds is a GAME CHANGER.

It's the perfect midday snack OR the perfect "light dinner" OR the perfect weekend movie night snack.

for the corn:
8 corn cobs, husks removed but reserved
1 tablespoon kosher salt
1 bunch cilantro

for the sauce:
¼ cup guajillo powder
¼ cup Chile lime seasoning
1 tablespoon ancho powder
1 teaspoon cayenne pepper
1 tablespoon kosher salt
½ cup lime juice

for serving and assembling:
1 cup mayonnaise
¼ cup Mexican crema
1 cup crumbled cotija cheese, plus more as needed
Parkay Squeeze Margarine
Lime wedges (optional)
Thick wooden skewers

elotes/ esquites

serves: **6 to 8**
prep time: **10 minutes**
cook time: **30 minutes**
total time: **40 minutes**

If I could only eat one snack for the rest of my life, this would be it. I grew up in Chicago where as soon as the weather got nice, we could hear the elotero riding his cart down the street honking his horn to let people know he was riding by. This was my version of the ice cream truck playing music. Eloteros serve elotes and esquites (and other street snacks) from a cart attached to a bike. I crave it almost every day, that's why there's a couple different recipes throughout this book inspired by elotes to give me that elote fix whenever I want it. For more about my love of elotes, see my love letter on page 194.

1 Fill a large pot with about 18 cups of water. Add the corn, salt, cilantro, and top it off with the removed husks from the corn. Set the pot over high heat and bring to a boil. Once boiling, reduce the heat to medium and cook for 20 minutes. Turn off the heat.

2 Prepare the sauce by adding all ingredients to a mixing bowl and mixing to combine. Thin out the sauce by adding 2 tablespoons of the water from the boiled corn. If the sauce is still too thick, add 1 or 2 more tablespoons. Taste the sauce and add more seasoning as needed. If you want it spicier add more cayenne pepper.

3 In a separate bowl mix together the mayo and the Mexican crema.

4 To assemble, grab a piece of corn, stick a skewer into the bottom, slather the cob evenly with the mayo/crema mixture, then spread over a layer of the Chile sauce mixture, coat all over with the crumbled cotija cheese, and lastly squirt over some of the Parkay margarine.

5 Enjoy as many as you'd like.

You can serve this on the cob or in a cup—if you serve it in a cup it's called esquites. To assemble in a cup, slice off the corn kernels from the cob, get a cup, add some of the mayo/crema mixture, some of the Chile sauce, add about 1 cup of the corn kernels, squeeze in some lime juice, and finish it off with more mayo/crema, cotija cheese, Chile sauce, and the parlay margarine.

2 tablespoons butter
2× 15.2 ounce (432g) cans corn, drained (2 cups frozen or fresh also works)
1 jalapeño, finely diced, optionally remove seeds for less spice
¼ small white onion, diced
2 garlic cloves, grated
1 tablespoon Tajín or chile-lime seasoning, plus more for garnish
1 teaspoon kosher salt
1 teaspoon black pepper
Juice of 2 limes, divided
1 bag sturdy tortilla chips, or homemade tortilla chips
2 cups shredded Oaxaca cheese, or any melting cheese such as mozzarella or pepper jack
½ cup cotija cheese, crumbled
¼ cup mayonnaise
¼ cup Mexican crema or sour cream
Chopped cilantro, for garnish

elote nachos

serves: **4 to 6**
prep time: **5 minutes**
cook time: **30 minutes**
total time: **35 minutes**

Street corn, esquites, elotes—put that deliciousness on everything and boy will I devour it! Something about the combination of corn, mayo, cotija, chile seasoning, and limon is just so addicting and always a favorite. I've been making a version of these nachos since I had my first apartment in college and my friends still request them to this day. If you're making these, maybe consider having extra ingredients in your pantry for a second batch because everyone will be asking for more.

1   To a large skillet over medium-high heat, add the butter.

2   Once the butter is melted, add the jalapeño, onion, and garlic. Cook for 1 to 2 minutes.

3   Add the corn and cook for 3 to 4 more minutes.

4   Add the chile-lime seasoning, salt, and pepper. Cook for 4 more minutes.

5   Turn off the heat and stir in the juice of one lime.

6   Preheat the oven to 350°F (180°C).

7   To assemble the nachos, get a half-sheet tray and arrange a single layer of tortilla chips on the bottom.

8   Sprinkle half of the cheese over the first layer of the tortilla chips.

9   Spoon half of the corn mixture on top of the cheese and finish it with half of the crumbled cotija cheese.

10 Repeat a second layer of the chips, the remaining cheese, and the remaining corn.

11 Place the tray of nachos in the oven and bake for 6 to 8 minutes or just until all the cheese has melted.

12 To serve the nachos, finish them with a drizzle of mayo and Mexican crema. Sprinkle over the remaining cotija cheese and squeeze over the juice of the second lime.

13 Top it off with freshly chopped cilantro for garnish and enjoy.

for the focaccia dough:
6 cups bread flour
1 packet active dry yeast
  (2¼ teaspoon)
1 tablespoon kosher salt
¼ cup extra-virgin olive oil

for the elote topping:
2 cups corn kernels, from 4
  ears of corn
1 jalapeño, thinly sliced
1 tablespoon Tajín or
  chile-lime seasoning
¼ cup extra-virgin olive oil

for baking & finishing:
½ cup extra-virgin olive oil
Crumbled cotija cheese

elote
foccacia

makes: **one foccacia**
prep time: **10 minutes**
cook time: **4 hours**
total time: **4 hours**

Ever since Claire Saffitz released her first cookbook, *Dessert Person,* I have been making focaccia whenever possible. I always thought making any kind of bread would be incredibly difficult, but shockingly, it's the opposite when it comes to focaccia. The dough itself comes together in a single mixing bowl—you don't even need a stand mixer. The hardest part is waiting for the yeast to work and make the dough rise. It's the best type of bread to snack on or use for sandwiches, and this street corn-inspired topping takes it to the next level. This recipe calls for a lot of olive oil (you won't be eating it all yourself, or you can, so don't be alarmed).

make it into... *a regular focaccia or top it with your favorite flavors. Simply toss together fresh rosemary with thinly sliced garlic and lots of olive oil, top the focaccia with it as you would the elote topping.*

Covered well in foil or plastic wrap, the focaccia will keep for 3 to 4 days.

1   To a small measuring cup, add ½ cup warm water and stir in the instant yeast. Let it sit and activate for 5 minutes.

2   To a large mixing bowl, add the flour, the yeast mixture, 2½ cups more water, and the salt. Stir with a wooden spoon until well combined with no visible dry flour.

3   To a separate large bowl, add ¼ cup olive oil and swirl around to coat the sides. Add the dough, cover, and let rise in a warm place until doubled in size, about 2 hours.

4   Punch the dough down and do two sets of stretches: grab and raise the dough from two ends, letting it naturally fall back down. Turn the bowl halfway and do the same stretching method again.

5   To a sheet pan, add ½ cup olive oil and spread it to coat the entire bottom.

6   Add in the dough and stretch it out as much as you can to the ends (you won't get it all the way). Cover again and let rest another 30 minutes.

7   After 30 minutes continue stretching out the dough to the edges. Cover and let rest and rise an additional 45 minutes to 1 hour.

8   During this final rise, mix the elote topping: add all ingredients to a bowl and stir to combine.

9   Preheat the oven to 450°F (230°C).

10   After the final rise, dimple the dough all over the surface, using your fingertips, and top with the elote mixture.

11   Bake the focaccia for 20 to 25 minutes or until perfectly crispy and golden brown on the bottom.

12   After baking, sprinkle the cotija cheese all over the top of the focaccia.

13   To serve, I like to cut the focaccia into squares using kitchen scissors. It's best served warm, but room temperature is also great.

for the sauce:
1½ cups sour cream
Juice of 1 lime
1 cup cilantro
1 teaspoon kosher salt
1 teaspoon black pepper

for the fritters:
2× 15.2 ounce (432g) cans
 corn, drained
1 pound (454g) bacon,
 sliced into chunks
2 jalapeños, finely chopped

4 green onions, thinly sliced
1× 8.5 ounce (240g) box
 Jiffy Cornbread Mix
2 large eggs
1 teaspoon black pepper
1 teaspoon garlic powder
8 ounces (454g) cheddar
 cheese, grated
Oil, for frying
Crumbled cotija cheese, for
 garnish

special equipment:
Blender

jalapeño popper fritters

serves: **6 as a main, 8 as an appetizer**
prep time: **5 minutes**
cook time: **1 hour**
total time: **1 hour 5 minutes**

I don't know about you, but I freaking love anything jalapeño popper-inspired. Bacon, cheese, and spicy jalapeños—what could be bad about that? Essentially, these fritters are another excuse to be able to say you had jalapeño poppers for dinner. Serve them as an appetizer for a party or make them the main event of any weekday dinner by serving with Chipotle Chicken (see page 153) or Green Spaghetti (see page 135).

Since we are frying in batches, I like to keep the fried fritters in my air fryer set to 200°F (95°C) to keep them warm.

1 To make the sauce add all ingredients to a blender. Blend until fully combined. Taste and add extra lime juice, salt, or pepper as needed. Pour the sauce into a bowl and refrigerate until ready to use.

2 Add the bacon to a large sauté pan set over medium-high heat. Cook the bacon, stirring frequently, until it gets crispy, 7 to 10 minutes.

3 Once crispy, transfer the bacon to a paper towel–lined plate to absorb any excess fat.

4 To a large mixing bowl, add the corn, bacon, jalapeños, green onions, cornbread mix, eggs, salt, pepper, garlic powder, and shredded cheese. Mix until fully combined.

5 To the same pan where you cooked the bacon, remove the excess bacon fat (save for another use if you'd like). Add enough oil to cover the bottom of the pan by at least ½ an inch and set it over medium heat.

6 Once hot, working in batches, use a 1-cup measuring cup to add the fritter mixture into the hot oil. Slightly flatten with the bottom of the cup once in the pan.

7 Fry the fritters for 2 to 3 minutes on the first side. Once slightly golden on the bottom, carefully flip them over.

8 Cook for another 3 to 4 minutes on the other side. Once golden, flip over one more time and cook for an additional 1 to 2 minutes.

9 Once cooked, remove from the pan and place on a paper towel–lined plate or baking sheet with a wire rack.

10 Continue until all fritters are fried.

11 Serve with dollops of the cilantro-lime crema and a sprinkling of the cotija cheese.

for the fried chicken:
2 pounds (907g) boneless, skinless chicken thighs
1 tablespoon, plus 1 teaspoon paprika
1 tablespoon, plus 1 teaspoon guajillo chile powder
1 tablespoon, plus 1 teaspoon onion powder
1 tablespoon, plus 1 teaspoon garlic powder
1 tablespoon, plus 1 teaspoon salt
1 tablespoon, plus 1 teaspoon black pepper
2 cups buttermilk
2 cups all-purpose flour
½ cup cornstarch
Oil, for frying

for the waffles:
1 cup all-purpose flour
1 cup cornmeal
1 tablespoon baking powder
1 teaspoon kosher salt
2 tablespoons sugar
2 tablespoons honey
2 eggs
4 tablespoons unsalted butter, melted
1½ cups buttermilk
Cooking oil spray

for the sauce:
2 tablespoons unsalted butter
½ cup honey
½ cup chipotle sauce
1 garlic clove, grated
2 teaspoons kosher salt

special equipment:
Waffle maker

honey chipotle chicken + waffles

serves: **4**
prep time: **10 minutes**
cook time: **1 hour 20 minutes**
total time: **1 hour 30 minutes (plus 1 hour for marinating)**

The first time I heard of chicken and waffles I thought to myself, *"What is that craziness? Give it to me now!!!"* Without a doubt, I knew I'd love the sweet and salty combination of crispy fried chicken with waffles and syrup. Obviously, I've added a spicy touch to the flavor profile by making a honey-chipotle sauce situation for these.

make it into... *a chicken and waffles sandwich by sandwiching a piece of fried chicken in between two waffles.*

1 To a large mixing bowl add the chicken thighs, 1 tablespoon each of the paprika, guajillo powder, onion powder, garlic powder, salt, and pepper, along with the buttermilk. Stir to combine. Cover and refrigerate for 1 hour to marinate.

2 To a second large mixing bowl, add in all the ingredients for the waffles and whisk them to fully combine.

3 Turn on your waffle maker, spray both top and bottom with the cooking spray, and pour in enough of the batter to fill it up. Cook waffles for about 5 to 6 minutes each. When cooked, set them on a sheet pan and continue cooking the rest of the waffles, spraying your waffle maker with more spray as needed.

4 Once all the waffles are cooked, I like to place the sheet pan in the oven at 250°F (120°C) to keep them warm.

5 Prepare the coating for the chicken by mixing the flour, cornstarch, and the remaining 1 teaspoon each of the seasonings.

6 Prepare the sauce by adding the 2 tablespoons of unsalted butter to a small saucepan set over medium heat. Once melted add in the honey, chipotle sauce, garlic, and salt. Stir to combine and cook on medium heat for 6 minutes, stirring constantly. Reduce heat to the lowest setting to stay warm until ready to serve.

7 To a large frying pan set over medium heat, add enough oil to fill up the pan with about ½ inch of oil.

8 To coat the chicken, remove from the buttermilk mixture, letting the excess drip off. Pass each piece through the flour mixture, making sure to pat it to fully coat. Set aside on a sheet tray and continue coating the rest of the chicken.

9 In batches, fry the chicken thighs: fry for 3 to 4 minutes on the first side, flip over, and fry for an additional 3 to 4 minutes. Keep an eye on the heat and adjust as needed since the temperature of the oil will change as chicken is added. Place on a paper towel–lined tray to soak up excess oil.

10 Continue frying the chicken in batches until it's all cooked.

11 Serve the chicken on top of the waffles and drizzle with the honey-chipotle sauce.

3 pounds baby potatoes (1 kg), washed
¼ cup, plus 1 tablespoon tomato bouillon
1 cup oil of choice
15 dried chiles de árbol, stems removed

4 dried guajillo peppers, stems and seeds removed
½ small white onion
5 garlic cloves
¾ cups lime juice

◇◇◇◇◇◇◇◇◇◇◇◇◇◇◇◇◇◇◇◇◇◇◇◇◇◇◇◇◇◇◇◇◇◇

papas enchiladas

serves: 8 to 10
prep time: 5 minutes
cook time: 25 minutes
total time: 30 minutes

These potatoes are ADDICTING. They're hella spicy but so delicious. As we like to say, it's the type of spicy that keeps you going back for more. They're the perfect party appetizer.

1   To a large soup pot set over high heat, add about 10 cups of water and bring to a boil.

2   Once boiling, add ¼ cup tomato bouillon and slowly add the potatoes to avoid splashing. Boil the potatoes until fork tender, 12 to 15 minutes.

3   While the potatoes boil, set a large frying pan over medium heat and add the oil.

4   Once hot, add the dried chiles and fry until toasted, 45 to 60 seconds. Turn off the heat.

5   Add the fried chiles to your blender along with the white onion, garlic, lime juice, and the remaining 1 tablespoon tomato bouillon. Blend until smooth, about 30 seconds.

6   With the blender on low speed and the top circle of your blender lid removed, slowly drizzle 1 cup of the oil used to fry the chiles. The oil will slightly thicken the sauce when you add it in.

7   Add the cooked potatoes to a bowl, pour in the blended chile sauce, and mix to combine.

8   Serve hot or at room temperature.

◇◇◇◇◇◇◇◇◇◇◇◇◇◇◇◇◇◇◇◇◇◇◇◇◇◇◇◇◇◇◇◇◇◇

These potatoes are SPICY, so proceed with caution

For less spice, double up on the guajillo chiles and reduce the amount of chiles de árbol to 3 or 5.

1 bag frozen waffle fries
Cooking oil spray
7 ounces (200g) Mexican
  chorizo
½ small white onion, finely
  diced
1 poblano pepper, stems
  and seeds removed, diced
4 tablespoons unsalted
  butter
¼ cup all-purpose flour

½ teaspoon garlic powder
½ teaspoon onion powder
½ teaspoon paprika
1 teaspoon kosher salt
1 teaspoon black pepper
2 cups beef broth
1 cup cheese curds
Chopped cilantro, for
  garnish
Pickled Red Onions (see
  page 51), for garnish

chorizo poutine

serves: **4 to 6**
prep time: **10 minutes**
cook time: **35 minutes**
total time: **45 minutes**

The first time I had poutine was at Disney World and, no surprise, I absolutely loved it. You can't go wrong with crispy fries loaded with gravy and cheese. Obviously, I found a way to add my go-to Mexican flavors with chorizo, diced poblano peppers, and pickled red onions to brighten everything up. Traditionally you'd use regular French fries, but using frozen waffle fries allows you to make this dish more of a shareable-type appetizer.

1   Prepare the waffles fries. Add them to a sheet pan, spray with oil, and cook according to package instructions. I usually aim to cook them an extra 3 to 5 minutes for crispier fries.

2   To a large sauté pan set over medium heat, add the chorizo and cook while breaking it into smaller pieces for 4 to 5 minutes.

3   Add the onion and poblano pepper and cook for another 5 to 6 minutes or until the onion has softened. Remove from the pan and set aside.

4   To the same pan add the butter. Once melted, add the flour and spices. Whisk until you see no more dry flour.

5   Slowly whisk in the beef broth. Reduce heat to low and simmer for at least 8 minutes or until the fries are ready.

6   To assemble, start with a layer of fries, scatter over half of the cheese curds, pour over half of the gravy, scatter over half of the chorizo. Continue with a second layer of fries, cheese curds, gravy, and the remaining chorizo.

7   Garnish and serve the poutine with cilantro and pickled red onions.

If using cheese that isn't cheese curds, you can bake the assembled fries at 350ºF (180ºC) for 8 to 10 minutes.

1 cup extra-virgin olive oil
2 garlic cloves
4 shallots, thinly sliced
5 dried chiles de árbol
1 tablespoon Maggi Jugo
1 tablespoon
  Worcestershire sauce
1 orange, juiced
½ cup lime juice
½ cup soy sauce
¼ small red onion, thinly
  sliced
2 serrano peppers, thinly
  sliced
2 ribeye steaks
Kosher salt
Black pepper, to taste
1 avocado, thinly sliced
½ cup roughly chopped
  cilantro

special equipment
Blender

ribeye aguachile

serves: **4 to 6**
prep time: **10 minutes**
cook time: **35 minutes**
total time: **45 minutes**

I started seeing ribeye aguachile on restaurant menus in South Texas a couple years ago. I thought it was weird but if you know me, I'll always try the weird stuff at least once before making a real judgment call. And as it turns out, this is one of my favorite things to get when it's on the menu. The warm, fatty steak with the spicy, acidic sauce is such an incredible combination.

1 To a frying pan set over medium heat, add the olive oil. Once hot, add the garlic cloves and fry until golden brown, about 4 to 5 minutes. Remove and set aside.

2 In the same oil, add the thinly sliced shallots and fry until golden brown and starting to crisp, 8 to 12 minutes. Transfer to a paper towel–lined plate and season with salt.

3 Make the aguachile sauce by adding the fried garlic, chiles de árbol, Maggi Jugo, Worcestershire sauce, orange juice, lime juice, and soy sauce to a blender. Blend until fully combined, 20 to 30 seconds.

4 Pour the aguachile sauce into a bowl, add in the thinly sliced red onion and serrano peppers, plus 2 tablespoons of the olive oil used to fry the shallots. Mix to combine and set aside.

5 Set a large frying pan or cast-iron skillet over medium heat.

6 Season the steaks liberally with salt and pepper.

7 Cook the steaks to medium rare: sear on the first side for 3 to 4 minutes, flip them over, and cook for an additional 3 to 4 minutes. For a more well-done steak, cook for 5 to 6 minutes per side. Let the steaks rest on a cutting board for 15 minutes before slicing.

8 Slice the steaks into thin ½-inch strips.

9 To serve, plate the steaks on a serving tray and pour over the aguachile sauce with the onion and serrano. Place the thinly sliced avocado around the plate with the steak and top it all off with the crispy fried shallots and the chopped cilantro.

10 Serve warm or at room temperature.

mole

When you add the mole to the pot, be wary of it splattering all over the place due to the heat of the pot. Have your lid nearby to cover immediately if it starts to splatter.

serves: **4 to 6, with extra mole sauce left over**
prep time: **30 minutes**
cook time: **2 hours 30 minutes**
total time: **3 hours**

Growing up, I was convinced I hated mole, which is probably one of the most iconic and beloved Mexican recipes ever. But recently, I discovered my love for it after going to a mole festival in Chicago. All the moles were made completely from scratch—up until then I had only ever had mole made from store-bought mole paste. I beg you, if you've never made mole from scratch, try it once. I know it seems intimidating because of the extremely long list of ingredients, but if you take the time to measure every ingredient into separate dishes before you even start cooking then the entire process is quite easy. This makes a lot of sauce, so freeze the leftover mole to use at a later date.

½ cup lard
10 dried guajillo peppers, stems and seeds removed
5 dried ancho peppers, stems and seeds removed
6 dried chiles de árbol, stems removed
2 corn tortillas (for homemade see page 24 or store-bought)
1 bolillo
½ cup salted peanuts
¼ cup almonds
¼ cup pumpkin seeds

¼ cup sesame seeds
¼ cup raisins
1 teaspoon whole cumin seeds
4 whole cloves
½ teaspoon whole peppercorns
6 garlic cloves
1 small white onion, roughly chopped
2 roma tomatoes
2 tomatillos, husks removed and washed
6 Maria cookies
8 cups chicken broth

4 to 6 pounds (2 to 3 kg) bone-in, skin-on chicken (I use a mix of chicken legs and thighs)
2 teaspoons kosher salt
2 teaspoons crushed black pepper
2 tablespoons avocado oil
2 disks Mexican chocolate
4 ounces (113g) piloncillo or ½ cup brown sugar
¼ cup creamy peanut butter

1   To a large frying pan set over medium heat, add the lard.

2   In batches, start frying the dried chiles. First, fry the guajillo chiles for 60 to 90 seconds. Transfer to a heat-proof bowl. Next, fry the ancho chiles for 60 to 90 seconds, then transfer to the bowl with guajillo chiles. Lastly, fry the chiles de árbol for 45 to 60 seconds and transfer to the same bowl. Pour boiling water into the bowl to submerge the peppers and cover. Let soak for 15 to 20 minutes.

3   In the same frying pan, fry the corn tortillas until crispy, about 2 minutes, the remove and set aside. Fry the bolillo until crispy, about 2 minutes, and set aside.

4   To the same pan, add all the nuts, seeds, onion, garlic, and spices, stirring frequently. Fry for about 6 minutes. Remove from the pan and set aside.

5   Add the tomatoes and tomatillos and cook until they begin to char all over, about 6 minutes. Remove and set aside.

6   To a blender, add the fried ingredients and the rehydrated chiles, along with the Maria cookies, 1 cup of the chile-soaking water, and some of the chicken broth. Add more broth as needed to create a smooth sauce. Work in batches if needed. Set aside.

7   Season the chicken all over with salt and pepper.

8   To a Dutch oven or large heavy bottom pot set over medium-high heat, add the avocado oil.

9   Once hot, work in batches to sear the chicken for 3 to 4 minutes on each side, or until the skin is golden brown. Remove from the pot and set aside. The chicken will still be raw but will finish cooking later.

10 Reduce the heat to medium and add the chicken broth to the Dutch oven. Use your spoon to scrape off the stuck-on bits from the bottom of the pot.

11 Reduce the heat to low and pour in the blended mole sauce. Stir to fully combine the chicken broth with the mole.

12 Raise the heat back up to medium. Add the Mexican chocolate, piloncillo, and creamy peanut butter, stirring every minute or so. Cook the sauce until the chocolate and piloncillo are fully melted and incorporated; the piloncillo will take longer to melt than the chocolate, about 12 to 15 minutes.

13 Once the piloncillo is fully melted, add the chicken back into the pot, along with any juices that accumulated at the bottom of the plate.

14 Cover, reduce heat to low, and cook, stirring every 3 to 5 minutes to make sure nothing is sticking/burning to the bottom of the pot.

15 Simmer on low until the chicken is cooked through, about 2 hours.

16 To serve, plate the pieces of chicken with a side of Mexican red rice and some extra mole sauce on top.

Mole isn't just for serving with chicken and rice. I always make big batches of it because you can easily freeze it to then use for many other recipes like these. None of these recipes have set measurements, they are meant to be quick and dirty.

Corn Tortillas (for homemade see page xx or store-bought)
Oil, for frying
Shredded cooked chicken
Mole Sauce (see page 212)
Queso fresco
Mexican crema
Pickled Red Onions (see page 51)

Mole Sauce (see page 212)
Tortilla chips
Fried eggs
Queso fresco
Mexican Crema
Pickled Red Onions (see page 51)
Salsa macha

enmoladas

Warm up the mole in a saucepan set over medium heat. To a frying pan set over medium heat, add some oil and fry the tortillas for 20 to 30 seconds per side. Dip them in the mole sauce, place on a plate, add shredded chicken, and roll them up. Continue with as many tortillas as you'd like to make. Top with more mole sauce, Mexican crema, crumbled queso fresco, and pickled red onions.

chilaquiles

Add the mole to a frying pan set to medium heat, add about ¼ cup water to loosen up. Once hot add in the tortilla chips and simmer for 1 to 2 minutes. Plate up the chilaquiles and serve with fried eggs and garnish with crumbled queso fresco, Mexican crema, pickled red onions and salsa macha.

mole matrix

1 ball fresh or frozen pizza dough
Mole sauce (see page 212)
Shredded cooked chicken
Shredded Chihuahua cheese
Queso fresco
Mexican crema
Salsa macha
Pickled Red Onions (see page 51)

pizza

Preheat the oven to 375°F (190°C). Spray a baking sheet with oil and spread out the pizza dough onto the baking sheet. Spread some mole on the bottom of the dough, top it off with some of the shredded chicken and sprinkle all over with shredded Chihuahua cheese. Bake for 15 to 18 minutes or until the cheese is bubbly and the crust is crispy. Top off the baked pizza with salsa macha, Mexican crema, crumbled queso fresco, and pickled red onions.

1 Ribeye or New York Strip Steak
Mole Sauce (see page 212)
Pickled Red Onions (see page 51)
Tortillas (for homemade see pages 23 and 24 or store-bought), for serving

steak

Cook the steak to your desired doneness. Serve on a bed of warmed up mole sauce and tortillas on the side.

postres y bebidas

mazapan iced coffee.................. 218

horchata.. 221

mexican chocolate almond
    croissants.....................................222

arroz con leche y mango...........225

strawberry matcha tres
    leches cake................................. 226

pan de elote 229

empanadas de pina................. 230

chocoflan 231

1 mazapan candy, plus more for garnish
1 teaspoon maple syrup (optional)
1 shot espresso or ⅓ cup coffee concentrate
½ cup to ¾ cup milk of choice (I tend to use whole milk)
Ice, for serving
Sweet Cold Foam, for garnish, optional

mazapan iced coffee

serves: **1**
prep time: **none**
cook time: **10 minutes**
total time: **10 minutes**

Writing this cookbook has turned me into a coffee lover. I spent many days going to different coffee shops to just sit down and write. At every coffee shop I'd try to get a different drink just to expand my horizons. I'm still no pro, but finally investing in my own espresso machine has made me experiment more with my drinks at home. This is one of those I keep going back to. Mazapan is a peanut-forward Mexican candy, they're delicious and notorious for being very fragile, so crumbling it up into pieces to make this drink shouldn't be an issue.

1 Crumble up the mazapan candy into the bottom of an espresso glass or coffee cup.

2 Add in the teaspoon of maple syrup, if using.

3 Brew your shot of espresso over the broken up mazapan and maple syrup. Stir together to fully combine the mazapan and syrup into the espresso. Allow to cool for 5 minutes.

4 Fill up a tall glass with ice.

5 Pour in the milk of your choice.

6 Pour the Mazapan-espresso mixture over the icy milk.

7 If using, top off the drink with cold foam.

8 Finish it off by crumbling more mazapan over the top.

2 cups long-grain white rice
3 cinnamon sticks
1 teaspoon vanilla bean
  paste or pure vanilla
  extract

1× 14 ounce (396 ml) can
  sweetened condensed
  milk
2 cups whole milk

special equipment
Blender

horchata

makes: **1 extra-large pitcher**
prep time: **4 hours**
cook time: **10 minutes**
total time: **4 hours and 10 minutes**

Horchata is one of the greatest drinks of all time. If it's on the menu, I'm getting it. So naturally, I had to learn how to make it at home (and the best part is how simple it is to prepare). At some restaurants they either make it too thick, overly sweet, or add way too much cinnamon. Making it at home allows you to control the final flavor.

1 Add the rice and cinnamon sticks to a large bowl and pour in 4 cups of boiling water.

2 Cover with a lid or plastic wrap and let it steep for at least 4 hours.

3 Remove two of the cinnamon sticks and add the rice, water, and remaining stick of cinnamon to a blender.

4 Add in the vanilla bean paste and sweetened condensed milk and blend until fully combined and smooth, about 1 minute.

5 Using a fine-mesh strainer, pour the blended rice mixture into an extra-large pitcher. If there's a large amount of pulp left over, you can blend it again with another cup of water and then add it to the pitcher.

6 Add the milk and 3 cups of cold water to the pitcher and stir well to combine.

7 Taste the horchata. If you want it sweeter, you can add in more sweetened condensed milk or stir in sugar a ¼ cup at a time until you've reached your desired sweetness.

8 Serve the horchata in tall glasses over ice.

1 cup granulated sugar
1 tablespoon chocolate
  tequila cream liqueur
  (optional)
1 cup almond flour
½ cup brown sugar
8 tablespoons (113g)
  unsalted butter, at room
  temperature
2 eggs
1 disk Mexican chocolate,
  plus more for garnish

⅓ cup all-purpose flour
½ teaspoon kosher salt
1 teaspoon vanilla bean
  paste
8 day-old croissants
1 cup sliced almonds
¼ cup powdered sugar

special equipment
Electric hand mixer

mexican chocolate almond croissants

makes: 8 croissants
prep time: 5 minutes
cook time: 40 minutes
total time: 45 minutes

I had my first almond croissant about two years ago, and since then I get one every time I see it on a menu. I'm not typically a big baker, so when coming up with dessert recipes for this book, I knew I had to find some way to Mexican-ize the almond croissant. That's how the Mexican chocolate-almond croissant was born. Mexican chocolate doesn't have much sweetness, so this is perfect if you don't like your desserts too sugary. Enjoy con un cafecito pal chisme con las tias to end the day.

1 To a saucepan set over medium heat, add the granulated sugar, 1 cup of water, and the tequila liqueur, if using. Bring to a simmer and cook, stirring constantly, until all the sugar has dissolved (about 4 minutes). You have now made a simple syrup. Take it off the heat and set aside for later.

2 In a large nonstick skillet set over medium-low heat, add the almond flour. Stirring constantly, toast the almond flour until it has darkened in color, 2 to 3 minutes. Take off the heat and dump it onto a plate to stop the cooking and avoid burning.

3 To a large mixing bowl, add the brown sugar and the butter.

4 Using a hand mixer, start on slow speed and work up to a medium-high speed. Whip the sugar and butter until fully combined.

5 Once combined, add in one egg and mix until combined, then add in the second egg and mix until combined.

6 Mexican chocolate comes in a large disk. Place it on a cutting board and, using a knife, start shaving it down until it's turned into a powder.

7 Add the toasted almond flour, Mexican chocolate, salt, and vanilla bean paste to the bowl. Mix until combined and you no longer see any flour.

8 Preheat the oven to 350°F (180°C).

9 Slice the croissants in half.

10 Using a pastry brush or small spoon, coat both cut sides of the croissants with the simple syrup—be generous and use all the syrup for the croissants.

11 Divide the chocolate almond mixture in half.

12 Spread half of the chocolate almond mixture onto half of each of the croissants and close them up.

13 Spread the remaining chocolate almond mixture on top of each croissant.

14 Top off each of the croissants with some of the sliced almonds.

15 Spray cookie sheets with cooking spray or parchment paper.

16 Place the croissants on the cookie sheets.

17 Bake for 22 to 25 minutes.

18 Immediately garnish them with a dusting of powdered sugar and grate some more Mexican chocolate on top.

19 Serve warm or at room temperature.

20 The croissants will keep at room temperature for 3 to 4 days.

1 cup jasmine rice
1 teaspoon kosher salt
1 stick of cinnamon
3 cups whole milk
1× 14 ounce (396 ml) can sweetened condensed milk

1× 12 ounce (354 ml) can evaporated milk
2 teaspoons vanilla bean paste
Diced mango, for serving

arroz con leche y mango

serves: **8**
prep time: **5 minutes**
cook time: **40 minutes**
total time: **45 minutes**

Growing up, I'd always make my mom buy those single-serving-sized cups of rice pudding at the store because it's one of the few things she'd never make. I loved it so much that we always had to have it in the fridge. Making it at home is so easy, and topping it with fresh mango (or any other fruit you prefer) lightens it up, allowing you to have a much larger bowl without feeling guilty about it.

1 To a large sauté pan set over medium heat, add the rice, 3 cups water, salt, and cinnamon stick.

2 Stirring every minute or so, cook the rice until it has absorbed most of the water but some still remains. This should take about 10 minutes.

3 Add in the milk, sweetened condensed milk, evaporated milk, and vanilla bean paste.

4 Cook, stirring every couple of minutes so that nothing sticks/burns at the bottom of the pan. Continue cooking until the rice is fully cooked, about 30 minutes.

5 You can serve the arroz con leche warm, at room temperature, or cold.

6 Serve in bowls with diced-up mango.

The arroz con leche will still be a bit loose after 30 minutes, but will thicken up as it cools down.

for the cake:
1× 15.2 ounce (432g) box
   vanilla cake mix
3 eggs
½ cup vegetable oil
1 cup milk
3 tablespoons matcha
   powder
Cooking oil spray

for the tres leches:
2 cups whole milk
1× 14 ounce (396 ml) can
   sweetened condensed
   milk
1× 12 ounce (354 ml) can
   evaporated milk
1 teaspoon vanilla bean
   paste or pure vanilla
   extract

for the frosting:
1 pound (450g)
   strawberries, stems
   removed, plus more for
   garnish
1× 8 ounce (226g) block
   cream cheese, at room
   temperature
1½ cups heavy cream
2 cups (227g) powdered
   sugar
1 teaspoon kosher salt

special equipment
Skewer
Electric hand mixer
9 × 13 inch (22 × 33 cm)
   baking pan

strawberry matcha tres leches cake

makes: 9 × 13 inch (2 × 33cm) cake
prep time: 5 minutes
cook time: 40 minutes
total time: 45 minutes (plus soaking time)

My favorite cake of all time is a tres leches cake. There's nothing wrong with a traditional tres leches cake, but for the sake of this book, I wanted to go out of the box by introducing matcha powder. I'm currently obsessed with drinking iced matcha lattes, so this was a no-brainer. It's delicious and will have everyone hooked the second you start serving it because of the green color. The overnight soaking of the cake with the three milks mixture is imperative. Soak it for less than 8 hours and the milk will ooze out the second you cut into it.

1   Preheat the oven to 350°F (180°C).

2   To a large mixing bowl, add the cake mix, 3 eggs, vegetable oil, milk, and matcha powder. Mix until fully combined.

3   Spray a 9 × 13 inch (23 × 33 cm) baking pan with nonstick cooking spray. Pour in the cake mix and bake the cake according to the box instructions, about 30 minutes.

4   Remove the cake from the oven and let cool for about 30 minutes.

5   Using a 4-cup measuring cup, add all the tres leches ingredients. Whisk to fully combine.

6   Using a long, thin wooden skewer, poke holes all over the cake.

7   Leaving the cake in the pan, slowly pour over the three-milks mixture. Some of it may pool around on the edges of the pan, but the cake will slowly soak it in.

8   Cover the cake pan with aluminum foil, refrigerate, and let rest for at least 8 hours or overnight.

9   When ready to serve the cake, add the strawberries to a large mixing bowl. Use a potato masher to mash them down, letting some chunks remain.

10 To the mashed strawberries, add the cream cheese, heavy cream, powdered sugar, and salt. Using an electric hand mixer, whip the mixture until it has thickened, 5 to 7 minutes.

11 Add the frosting to the cake and spread into an even layer.

12 If desired, you can top the cake with slices of strawberries.

13 Serve and slice the cake from the pan.

Because of the mashed strawberries, the frosting won't get completely stiff as a whipped cream frosting would.

You can leave out the mashed strawberries from the frosting and simply slice them up to garnish the frosted cake.

make it into... *a traditional tres leches cake by simply omitting the matcha powder in the cake batter.*

Kernels from 4 corn cobs (about 2 cups corn kernels)

4 eggs

8 tablespoons (113g) unsalted butter

1× 14 ounce (396 ml) can sweetened condensed milk

1× 12 ounce (354 ml) can evaporated milk

1 tablespoon baking powder

1 tablespoon vanilla bean paste or pure vanilla extract

1 teaspoon kosher salt

¼ cup all-purpose flour

Cooking oil spray

for serving:
Dulce de leche
Vanilla ice cream

special equipment
Blender
8 × 8 inch (20 × 20 cm) baking dish

pan de elote

makes: **1 pan de elote**
prep time: **10 minutes**
cook time: **50 minutes**
total time: **1 hour**

This isn't your traditional pan de elote or cornbread. My tia helped me with this recipe, and at first, I thought I did something wrong because I'd never had cornbread like it. It tasted great but it wasn't necessarily a "bread"-like consistency. It's a mix between a custardy flan and bread pudding. When she came over to try it, she immediately said, *"Te quedo deli deli,"* aka, "It's so yummy, yummy." If you think you're not a baker, you will be with this recipe because it all gets blended together, poured into a baking dish, and baked. Can't get any easier than that!

1 To a small frying pan set over medium heat, add the butter. Once melted, stir continuously and keep cooking until the butter has browned, 4 to 5 minutes. Immediately pour the browned butter into a small bowl to avoid burning. Let it cool down for a few minutes.

2 Preheat the oven to 375°F (190°C).

3 To your blender, add the corn, eggs, browned butter, sweetened condensed milk, evaporated milk, baking powder, vanilla, salt, and flour. Blend on a medium-low speed until combined but not completely smooth to still have some chunks of corn in there.

4 Spray a square 8 × 8 inch (20 × 20 cm) baking dish with cooking spray.

5 Pour the batter into the baking dish then bake for 36 to 40 minutes.

6 Remove the cake from the oven and let cool for 15 minutes before serving.

7 I like to cut into squares and top with a scoop of ice cream and a drizzle of dulce de leche.

for the filling:
1½ cups pineapple preserves
1 egg yolk
1 pinch ground cloves
½ teaspoon kosher salt
1 teaspoon pure vanilla bean paste or pure vanilla extract

for the dough:
2¾ cups (330g) all-purpose flour, plus more if needed
16 tablespoons (226g) unsalted butter, at room temperature

1× 8 ounce (226g) block cream cheese, at room temperature
1 teaspoon kosher salt

for the coating:
⅔ cup granulated sugar
1 teaspoon ground cinnamon

special equipment:
Tortilla press
1 zip-top plastic bag, cut open

empanadas de pina

makes: **30 to 36 empanadas**
prep time: **5 minutes**
cook time: **55 minutes**
total time: **1 hour**

There are many fillings out there for empanadas, but empanadas de pina are my weakness. I only found out a couple of years ago that there's cream cheese in the dough, which makes sense because they're so delicate and dissolve in your mouth. Be prepared for these to be gone immediately because it's hard to eat just one.

This recipe works great with the help of a second person— one person flattens out the empanada dough while the other person fills and closes them up.

If your dough seems too soft to work with, mix in a bit more flour 1 tablespoon at a time.

1 To a small bowl, add all the ingredients for the filling, stir to combine, and set aside.

2 To a large mixing bowl add the ingredients for the dough and start mixing by hand until a smooth dough forms (it should take 4 to 6 minutes).

3 Divide the dough into small, gumball-sized pieces.

4 Using a tortilla press and plastic bag for the dough, place the dough in between the plastic and flatten it down. It should be about 4 to 5 inches in diameter.

5 Place the dough disks on a clean surface in a single layer to avoid them sticking and continue flattening out the remaining dough balls.

6 Preheat the oven to 350°F (180°C).

7 To fill the empanadas, add about 1 tablespoon of filling to the middle of each dough disk, fold it in half like a taco, and crimp the edges closed. Use either a fork or crimp by hand. Continue filling all the empanadas.

8 Place the filled and folded empanadas on a parchment paper-lined baking tray.

9 Bake the empanadas for 12 to 15 minutes or until the bottom of the empanadas appear light golden.

10 While the empanadas are baking, mix the sugar and cinnamon together in a medium bowl.

11 Once the empanadas are cooked, immediately toss them in the cinnamon-sugar mixture to coat. If you wait until they've cooled down, the coating won't stick.

12 Serve warm or at room temperature.

learn how to crimp empanadas

make it into... *make the empanadas with a cajeta filling. Instead of the pineapple preserves, use canned dulce de leche mixed with an egg yolk as well and proceed with the recipe as written.*

for the chocolate cake:
1× 15.2 ounce (432g) box chocolate cake mix
1¼ cups whole milk
½ cup vegetable oil
3 eggs
Cooking oil spray

for the flan:
4 eggs
1× 14 ounce (396 ml) can sweetened condensed milk
1× 12 ounce (354 ml) can evaporated milk

1 tablespoon pure vanilla extract
1× 8 ounce (226g) block cream cheese, at room temperature

for topping:
1 cup dulce de leche
½ cup chopped pecans

special equipment:
Blender
Bundt cake pan
Roasting pan

chocoflan

makes: **1 cake**
prep time: **10 minutes**
cook time: **1 hour 20 minutes**
total time: **1 hour 30 minutes (plus cooling time)**

This is one of my favorite desserts to make as it's known as the impossible cake by a lot of people. That's because to bake it, you start by pouring the cake batter into a bundt pan, then you pour the flan mixture over the top. Once it's baked and you unmold it, the layers will be swapped. I'm not a scientist, I have zero idea how that works, but it works, and the result is so good.

1   Preheat the oven to 350°F (180°C).

2   Prepare the cake batter by adding all cake ingredients to a large bowl and mixing with a whisk until fully combined.

3   To your blender, add all ingredients for the flan and blend until completely smooth and combined, about 30 seconds.

4   Spray the bundt pan with cooking spray.

5   Pour the cake batter into the bottom of the bundt pan. Slowly pour the flan mixture over the cake batter. Cover with foil.

6   Put the filled bundt pan in the middle of the roasting pan and pour boiling hot water into the roasting pan. The water should come up about an inch on the sides of the bundt pan.

7   Bake the chocoflan for 65 to 75 minutes. Test for doneness by poking a hole through the cake with a wooden skewer, if it comes out clean it's ready.

8   Remove the foil and let the cake cool down for about 1 hour.

9   To unmold, place a large serving tray over the bundt pan and carefully flip it over. Gently remove the bundt pan.

10   Garnish the chocoflan by drizzling the dulce de leche over the top, letting it drip down the sides. Top with the crushed pecans.

index

A

achiote paste, in Al Pastor, 89
Al Pastor, 89
American cheese
  Cheeseburger Flautas, 151
  Mexican Smash Burgers, 113
  Tater Tot Breakfast Tacos, 36
American Pizza, 186
ancho peppers/chiles
  Al Pastor, 89
  Barbacoa, 46
  Birria, 184
  Mole, 212
  Pozole Rojo, 172
anchovies, in Poblano Caesar Salad, 179
Arroz con Leche y Mango, 225
artichoke hearts, in Spinach Artichoke Quesadillas, 144
Asian pear, in Bulgogi Tacos, 99
avocado(s)
  avocado salsa, 50
  Chicken Tortilla Soup, 167
  Chilaquiles Burger, 114
  Chipotle Avocado BLT, 109
  Coconut Ceviche, 78
  Crispy Panela with Creamy Avocado Dip, 74
  Fried Egg Tacos, 35
  Guac Egg Salad Tacos, 94
  Mexican Smash Burgers, 113
  Queso Panela Aguachile, 77
  Ribeye Aguachile, 210
  Salsa Verde Cruda, 57
  Sloppy Jose's, 110
  Snacking Tortillas, 24
  Tacos de Fideo Seco, 93
Avocado Jalapeño Dip
  recipe, 70
  Tater Tot Breakfast Tacos, 36

B

bacon
  Chipotle Avocado BLT, 109
  Frijoles Charros aka Cowboy Beans, 29
  Jalapeño Popper Fritters, 202
  Jalapeño Popper Tacos, 100
  Mexican Hot Dogs, 120
  Mexican Smash Burgers, 113
  Tater Tot Breakfast Tacos, 36
Barbacoa, 46
beans. See also Refried Beans
  Frijoles Charros aka Cowboy Beans, 29
  Green Chili, 175
  Milanesa de Res with, 152
  Pot of Pinto or Black Beans, 28
beef. See also ground beef; steak
  Barbacoa, 46
  Birria, 184
beer, in Salsa Borracha, 62
bell pepper
  Chicken Tortilla Soup, 167
  Picadillo, 90
  Red Rice, 25
  Sloppy Jose's, 110
berries
  Strawberry Guajillo Jam, 32
  Strawberry Matcha Tres Leches Cake, 226
Birria
  recipe, 184
  recipes using, 186–187
breadcrumbs, in Milanesa de Res, 152. See also panko breadcrumbs
Bulgogi Tacos, 99
burgers
  Chilaquiles Burger, 114
  Mexican Smash Burgers, 113

C

cabbage. See also kimchi
  Chile-Lime Poke Bowls, 161
  Green Chili, 175
  Pozole Rojo, 172
cakes
  Chocoflan, 231
  Strawberry Matcha Tres Leches, 226
calabacitas
  Caldo de Albondigas, 168
  Chicken Tortilla Soup, 167
  Costra de Calabaza, 95
  Green Chili, 175
  Mexican Lasagna, 140
Caldo de Albondigas, 13, 168
Carne Asada
  recipe, 118
  recipes using, 120–121
Carnitas, 86
carrots
  Caldo de Albondigas, 168
  Chicken Tortilla Soup, 167
  Poblano Pot Pie, 158
carrots, from pickled jalapeños, in Avocado Jalapeño Dip, 70
chamoy, in Mango Chamoy Wings, 189
cheddar cheese
  Creamy Enchilada Soup with Grilled Cheese, 164
  Enchilada Dip, 69
  Jalapeño Popper Fritters, 202
  Tex-Mex Enchiladas, 148
cheese. See specific types of cheeses
Cheeseburger Flautas, 151
cheese curds, in Chorizo Poutine, 209
Cheese Stuffed Tortilla Chips, 73
Cheetos, in Chile-Lime Poke Bowls, 161
chicharrones (pork rinds)
  Frijoles Charros aka Cowboy Beans, 29
  Salsa de Chicharron, 65
chicken
  Cilantro Lime Roast Chicken, 154
  Enmoladas, 214
  Mole, 212
  Pizza with mole, 215
  Poblano Pot Pie, 158
chicken breasts
  Chicken Tortilla Soup, 167
  Chipotle Chicken, 153
  Mexican Chicken Parm, 157
  Poblano Caesar Salad, 179
  Pollo Asada, 129
  Spinach Artichoke Quesadillas, 144

chicken thighs
  Honey Chipotle
    Chicken & Waffles,
    205
  Pollo Asada, 129
  Taki's Chicken
    Sandwich, 104

chicken wings
  Mango Chamoy Wings,
    191
  Sweet & Spicy Macha
    Wings, 192
  Valentina Wings, 188

chihuahua cheese
  American Pizza, 186
  Cheese Stuffed Tortilla
    Chips, 73
  Chilaquiles Rojos, 43
  Chilaquiles Verdes, 42
  Chilaquiles with birria,
    186
  Egg Rolls, 187
  Mexican Pizza, 186
  Pizza with mole, 215
  Spinach Artichoke
    Quesadillas, 144
  Tortas, 121

chilaquiles, 40–43
  Chilaquiles Rojos, 43
  Chilaquiles Verdes, 42

Chilaquiles Burger, 114
Chilaquiles Divorciados, 43
Chilaquiles with birria, 186
Chilaquiles with mole, 214
Chile-Lime Poke Bowls,
  161
chile lime seasoning. See
  also Tajin
  Elotes/Esquites, 197
  Mango Chamoy Wings,
    191

chiles de arbol
  Birria, 184
  Enchiladas Rojas, 147
  Mango Chamoy Wings,
    189
  Mole, 212
  Papas Enchiladas, 206
  Pineapple Salsa Verde,
    55
  Pozole Rojo, 172
  Ribeye Aguachile, 210
  Salsa Borracha, 62
  Salsa de Chicharron, 65
  Salsa Roja, 52

chiles, dried. See ancho
  peppers/chiles; chiles
  de arbol; guajillo
  peppers, dried
chiles poblanos. See
  poblano peppers
Chiles Rellenos, 143
chili crisp, in Salsa Macha
  Marinated Goat
  Cheese, 66
Chili, Green, 175
Chipotle Avocado BLT, 109
Chipotle Chicken, 153
chipotle peppers in adobo
  Caldo de Albondigas,
    168
  Chipotle Chicken, 153
  Creamy Enchilada Soup
    with Grilled Cheese,
    164
  Pollo Asada, 129

chipotle sauce
  Chipotle Avocado BLT,
    109
  Honey Chipotle
    Chicken & Waffles,
    193
  Mexican Chicken Parm,
    157
  Sloppy Jose's, 110

Chocoflan, 231
chocolate, Mexican. See
  Mexican chocolate
chocolate tequila cream
  liqueur, in Mexican
  Chocolate Almond
  Croissants, 222
Chori-Queso Baked
  Spaghetti, 139
chorizo. See also Mexican
  chorizo
  Frijoles Charros aka
    Cowboy Beans, 29
  Sloppy Jose's, 110

Chorizo Poutine, 209
Cilantro-Lime Rice, 26
Cilantro Lime Roast
  Chicken, 154
Coconut Ceviche, 78
coconut flakes, in Sweet &
  Spicy Coconut Lobster
  (or Shrimp) Sandwich,
  106
coconut milk, in Coconut
  Ceviche, 78
Coffee, Mazapan Iced, 218

corn/corn cobs
  Caldo de Albondigas,
    168
  Chicken Tortilla Soup,
    167
  Elote Focaccia, 201
  Elote Nachos, 198
  Elote Potato Salad, 126
  Elotes/Esquites, 197
  Jalapeño Popper
    Fritters, 202
  Pan de Elote, 229
  Street Corn Ravioli, 136
  White Rice with Corn,
    26

cornmeal, in Honey
  Chipotle Chicken &
  Waffles, 193
Corn Tortillas
  Al Pastor, 89
  Barbacoa, 46
  Bulgogi Tacos, 99
  Caldo de Albondigas
    with, 168
  Carnitas, 86
  Cheeseburger Flautas,
    151
  Cheese Stuffed Tortilla
    Chips, 73
  Chilaquiles Burger, 114
  Chilaquiles Rojos, 43
  Chilaquiles Verdes, 42
  Costra de Calabaza, 95
  Enchiladas Rojas, 147
  Enmoladas, 214
  Fried Egg Tacos, 35
  Jalapeño Popper Tacos,
    100
  Migas, 39
  Mole, 212
  Picadillo, 90
  Pork Belly Kimchi
    Tacos, 96
  recipe, 24
  Spinach Artichoke
    Quesadillas, 144
  Tacos de Fideo Seco, 93
  Tex-Mex Enchiladas,
    148

Costra de Calabaza, 95
cotija cheese
  Elote Focaccia, 201
  Elote Nachos, 198
  Elote Potato Salad, 126
  Elotes/Esquites, 197

Jalapeño Popper
  Fritters, 202
Street Corn Ravioli, 136
Cowboy Beans (Frijoles
  Charros), 29
cream cheese
  Avocado Jalapeño Dip,
    70
  Chipotle Chicken, 153
  Chocoflan, 231
  Empanadas de Pina,
    230
  Enchilada Dip, 69
  Green Spaghetti, 135
  Jalapeño Popper Tacos,
    100
  Mexican Lasagna, 140
  Strawberry Matcha Tres
    Leches Cake, 226

Creamy Avocado Jalapeño
  Dip, 13
Creamy Enchilada Soup
  with Grilled Cheese,
  164
Crispy Panela with Creamy
  Avocado Dip, 74
Croissants, Mexican
  Chocolate Almond,
  222
croutons, in Poblano
  Caesar Salad, 179
cucumber
  Chile-Lime Poke Bowls,
    161
  Coconut Ceviche, 78
  Mexican-ish Greek
    Salad, 176
  Queso Panela
    Aguachile, 77
  Watermelon Feta Salad,
    123

D
dips
  Crispy Panela with
    Creamy Avocado
    Dip, 74
  Enchilada Dip, 69

dulce de leche
  Chocoflan, 231
  Pan de Elote, 229

E
edamame, in Chile-Lime
  Poke Bowls, 161
Egg Rolls, 187

eggs
    Caldo de Albondigas, 168
    Chilaquiles Burger, 114
    Chilaquiles Rojos, 43
    Chilaquiles Verdes, 42
    Chilaquiles with mole, 214
    Chiles Rellenos, 143
    Chocoflan, 231
    Fried Egg Tacos, 35
    Guac Egg Salad Tacos, 94
    Honey Chipotle Chicken & Waffles, 193
    Jalapeño Popper Fritters, 202
    Mexican Chicken Parm, 157
    Mexican Chocolate Almond Croissants, 222
    Migas, 39
    Milanesa de Res, 152
    Pan de Elote, 229
    Strawberry Matcha Tres Leches Cake, 226
    Tater Tot Breakfast Tacos, 36

Elote Focaccia, 201
Elote Nachos, 198
Elote Potato Salad, 126
elotes, about, 194
Elotes/Esquites, 197
Empanadas de Pina, 230
Enchilada Dip, 69
enchiladas
    Enchiladas Rojas, 147
    Tex-Mex Enchiladas, 148

Enchilada Sauce
    Creamy Enchilada Soup with Grilled Cheese, 164
    Enchilada Dip, 69
    Enchiladas Rojas, 147
    Sloppy Jose's, 110
    Tex-Mex Enchiladas, 148

Enmoladas, 214
equipment, 14
espresso, in Mazapan Iced Coffee, 218
evaporated milk

Arroz con Leche y Mango, 225
Chocoflan, 231
Pan de Elote, 229
Strawberry Matcha Tres Leches Cake, 226

F
feta cheese
    Mexican-ish Greek Salad, 176
    Watermelon Feta Salad, 123
fideo noodles
    Sopa de Fideo, 171
    Tacos de Fideo Seco, 93
fish and seafood
    Chile-Lime Poke Bowls, 161
    Coconut Ceviche, 78
    Sweet and Spicy Coconut Lobster (or Shrimp) Sandwich, 106
Flautas, Cheeseburger, 151
Flour Tortillas
    Barbacoa, 46
    Carnitas, 86
    Guac Egg Salad Tacos, 94
    Mexican Pizza, 186
    Migas, 39
    Pork Belly Kimchi Tacos, 96
    recipe, 23
    Snacking Tortillas, 24
    Spinach Artichoke Quesadillas, 144
    Tater Tot Breakfast Tacos, 36
Freddsters (food blog), 10
Fried Egg Breakfast Taco, 13
Fried Egg Tacos, 35
Fries, Carne Asada, 120
Frijoles Charros aka Cowboy Beans, 29
Fritters, Jalapeño Popper, 202

G
Garcia, Jaime, 10
garlic, grating, 19
giardiniera, Spicy Mortadella Sandwich served with, 107

ginger, fresh
    Birria, 184
    Bulgogi Tacos, 99
goat cheese
    Creamy Enchilada Soup with Grilled Cheese, 164
    Salsa Macha Marinated Goat Cheese, 66
gochugaru, in Bulgogi Tacos, 99
gochugaru pepper flakes
    Kimchi Pico de Gallo, 60
    Pork Belly Kimchi Tacos, 96
gochujang
    Bulgogi Tacos, 99
    Pork Belly Kimchi Tacos, 96
Green Chili, 175
Green Spaghetti, 135
Green Spaghetti sauce, in Mexican Chicken Parm, 157
Grilled Cheese
    with Birria, 187
    Cream Enchilada Soup with, 164
ground beef, 69
    Caldo de Albondigas, 168
    Cheeseburger Flautas, 151
    Chilaquiles Burger, 114
    Chori-Queso Baked Spaghetti, 139
    Enchilada Dip, 69
    Mexican Smash Burgers, 113
    Picadillo, 90
    Sloppy Jose's, 110
    Tex-Mex Enchiladas, 148
ground chicken/turkey
    Green Chili, 175
    Mexican Lasagna, 140
ground pork, in Green Chili, 175
guacamole
    Carne Asada Fries, 120
    Mexican Pizza, 186
Guac Egg Salad Tacos, 94
guajillo peppers, dried

Al Pastor, 89
Barbacoa, 46
Birria, 184
Chilaquiles Rojos, 43
Enchiladas Rojas, 147
Mole, 212
Papas Enchiladas, 206
Pozole Rojo, 172
Salsa Roja, 52

H
habanero peppers
    Habanero Salsa, 61
    Pickled Red Onions, 51
    Sweet & Spicy Coconut Lobster (or Shrimp) Sandwich, 106
ham, in Mexican Smash Burgers, 113
"Hay comida en la casa," 20
heavy cream
    Creamy Enchilada Soup with Grilled Cheese, 164
    Green Spaghetti, 135
    Poblano Pot Pie, 158
    Strawberry Matcha Tres Leches Cakes, 226
    Street Corn Ravioli, 136
hominy
    Green Chili, 175
    Pozole Rojo, 172
Honey Chipotle Chicken & Waffles, 205
Horchata, 221
Hot Dogs, Mexican, 120

I
ice cream, Pan de Elote with, 229
Iced Coffee, Mazapan, 218
ingredients, basic, 14

J
Jalapeño Popper Fritters, 202
Jalapeño Popper Tacos, 100
Jam, Strawberry Guajillo, 32
jasmine rice
    Arroz con Leche y Mango, 225
    Caldo de Albondigas, 168

Cilantro-Lime Rice, 26
White Rice with Corn, 26

Jiffy Cornbread Mix, in Jalapeño Popper Fritters, 202
Johnson-Reyes, Anjelah, 13

K
kewpie mayo, in Chile-Lime Poke Bowls, 161
kimchi
Kimchi Pico de Gallo, 60
Pork Belly Kimchi Tacos, 96

L
lard
Carnitas, 86
Flour Tortillas, 23
Mole, 212
Refried Beans, 29
Lasagna, Mexican, 140
lettuce
Cheeseburger Flautas, 151
Chipotle Avocado BLT, 109
Mexican Smash Burgers, 113
Picadillo, 90
Poblano Caesar Salad, 179
Taki's Chicken Sandwich, 1064
Tortas, 121
Loaded Papa Asada, 121
lobster tails, in Sweet & Spicy Coconut Lobster (or Shrimp) Sandwich, 106

M
Macha Peanut Noodles, 132
mango
Arroz con Leche y Mango, 225
Chile-Lime Poke Bowls, 161
Mango Chamoy Wings, 189
Mango Chamoy Wings, 191
Maria cookies, in Mole, 212

marinara sauce, in Chori-Queso Baked Spaghetti, 139
masa harina, in Corn Tortillas, 24
matcha powder, in Strawberry Matcha Tres Leches Cake, 226
mazapan candy, in Mazapan Iced Coffee, 218
Mexican Chicken Parm, 157
Mexican chocolate
Mexican Chocolate Almond Croissants, 222
Mole, 212
Mexican chorizo
Chori-Queso Baked Spaghetti, 139
Chorizo Poutine, 209
Tacos de Fideo Seco, 93
Mexican Coke, in Carnitas, 86
Mexican crema
Avocado Jalapeño Dip, 70
Chipotle Chicken, 153
Crispy Panela with Creamy Avocado Dip, 74
Elote Nachos, 198
Elotes/Esquites, 197
Green Spaghetti, 135
Mexican Lasagna, 140
Poblano Pot Pie, 158
Street Corn Ravioli, 136
Mexican hot dogs, 120
Mexican-ish Greek Salad, 176
Mexican Lasagna, 140
Mexican Pizza, 186
microplanes, 19
Migas, 39
Milanesa de Res, 152
Mole
recipe, 212
recipes using, 214–215
mortadella, in Spicy Mortadella Sandwich, 107
mozzarella cheese
Creamy Enchilada Soup with Grilled Cheese, 164

Elote Nachos, 198
Mexican Chicken Parm, 157
Muenster cheese
Chilaquiles Burger, 114
Chiles Rellenos, 143
Chori-Queso Baked Spaghetti, 139
Costra de Calabaza, 95
Creamy Enchilada Soup with Grilled Cheese, 164
Jalapeño Popper Tacos, 100
Mexican Chicken Parm, 157
Mexican Lasagna, 140
Mexican Smash Burgers, 113
Spicy Mortadella Sandwich, 107
Taki's Chicken Sandwich, 104

N
nacho cheese, in Loaded Papa Asada, 121
Nachos, Elote, 198
Not Spicy Restaurant-Style Salsa, 56
nuts
Chocoflan, 231
Macha Peanut Noodles, 132
Mexican Chocolate Almond Croissants, 222
Mole, 212
Sweet & Spicy Macha Wings, 192

O
Oaxaca cheese, in Elote Nachos, 198
orange
Carne Asada, 118
Carnitas, 86
Ribeye Aguachile, 210

P
Pan de Elote, 229
panko breadcrumbs
Crispy Panela with Creamy Avocado Dip, 74
Mexican Chicken Parm, 157

Sweet & Spicy Coconut Lobster (or Shrimp) Sandwich, 106
pantry ingredients, 14
Papas Enchiladas, 206
Parkay Squeeze Butter, in Elotes/Esquites, 197
Parmesan cheese, in Poblano Caesar Salad, 179
peanut butter
Macha Peanut Noodles, 132
Mole, 212
peas, in Poblano Pot Pie, 158
pepper jack cheese
Elote Nachos, 198
Taki's Chicken Sandwich, 104
Philadelphia Cream Cheese, 13. See also cream cheese
Picadillo
Chiles Rellenos, 143
recipe, 90
pickled jalapeños
Avocado Jalapeño Dip, 70
Mexican Smash Burgers, 113
Spicy Mortadella Sandwich, 107
Pickled Red Onions
Bulgogi Tacos, 99
Carne Asada Fries, 120
Chicken Tortilla Soup, 167
Chilaquiles, 186
Chilaquiles Rojos, 43
Chilaquiles Verdes, 42
Chilaquiles with mole, 214
Chile-Lime Poke Bowls, 161
Chorizo Poutine, 209
Enmoladas, 214
Green Chili, 175
Mexican Chicken Parm, 157
Pizza with mole, 215
recipe, 51
Steak with mole, 215
Pico de Gallo, 122

pineapple
  Al Pastor, 89
  Pineapple Salsa Verde, 55
  Sweet & Spicy Coconut Lobster (or Shrimp) Sandwich, 106

pineapple preserves, in Empanadas de Pina, 230

Pineapple Salsa Verde, 55

pinto beans. *See* beans

Pizza
  American Pizza, 186
  Mexican Pizza, 186
  with mole, 215

poblano peppers
  Chicken Tortilla Soup, 167
  Chiles Rellenos, 143
  Chorizo Poutine, 209
  Green Chili, 175
  Green Spaghetti, 135
  Mexican Lasagna, 140
  Poblano Caesar Salad, 179
  Poblano Pot Pie, 158
  roasting, 16

Poke Bowls, Chile-Lime, 161

Pollo Asada, 129

pork. *See also* bacon
  Al Pastor, 89
  Carnitas, 86
  Green Chili, 175
  Mexican Smash Burgers, 113
  Pork Belly Kimchi Tacos, 96
  Pozole Rojo, 172
  Spicy Mortadella Sandwich, 107

Pork Belly Kimchi Tacos, 96

potatoes
  Caldo de Albondigas, 168
  Cilantro Lime Roast Chicken, 154
  Elote Potato Salad, 126
  Loaded Papa Asada, 121
  Papas Enchiladas, 206
  Picadillo, 90
  Poblano Pot Pie, 158

Pot Pie, Poblano, 158

Pozole Rojo, 172

produce, 14

pumpkin seeds, in Mole, 212

Q
Quesadillas, Spinach Artichoke, 144

queso fresco
  Carne Asada Fries, 120
  Chicken Tortilla Soup, 167
  Chilaquiles Rojos, 43
  Chilaquiles Verdes, 42
  Chilaquiles with mole, 214
  Enchiladas Rojas, 147
  Enmoladas, 214
  Fried Egg Tacos, 35
  Green Chili, 175
  Green Spaghetti, 135
  Mexican Chicken Parm, 157
  Migas, 39
  Pizza with mole, 215
  Sloppy Jose's, 110
  Tacos de Fideo Seco, 93

queso panela
  Chiles Rellenos, 143
  Crispy Panela with Creamy Avocado Dip, 74
  Queso Panela Aguachile, 77

R
radishes
  Green Chili, 175
  Pozole Rojo, 172

raisins, in Mole, 212

ramen noodles, in Macha Peanut Noodles, 132

Ravioli, Street Corn, 136

red onions. *See* Pickled Red Onions

Red Rice, 25

Refried Beans
  Chilaquiles Rojos, 43
  Chilaquiles Verdes, 42
  Fried Egg Tacos, 35
  Migas, 39
  Picadillo, 90
  recipe, 29
  Tortas, 121

requeson, in Mexican Lasagna, 140

Ribeye Aguachile, 210

rice. *See also* jasmine rice
  Chipotle Chicken with, 153
  Horchata, 221
  Milanesa de Res with, 152
  Red Rice, 25
  Tex-Mex Enchiladas with, 148

ricotta cheese, in Mexican Lasagna, 140

Roma tomatoes
  Birria, 184
  Caldo de Albondigas, 168
  Chilaquiles Rojos, 43
  Chipotle Avocado BLT, 109
  Chipotle Chicken, 153
  Enchilada Dip, 69
  Frijoles Charros aka Cowboy Beans, 29
  Habanero Salsa, 61
  Kimchi Pico de Gallo, 60
  Mole, 212
  Not Spicy Restaurant-Style Salsa, 56
  Pico de Gallo, 122
  Red Rice, 25
  Refried Beans, 29
  Salsa Borracha, 62
  Salsa de Chicharron, 65
  Salsa Roja, 52
  Tex-Mex Enchiladas, 148

rotisserie chicken, in Poblano Pot Pie, 158

S
salads
  Elote Potato Salad, 126
  Mexican-ish Greek Salad, 176
  Poblano Caesar Salad, 179
  Watermelon Feta Salad, 123

salsa(s). *See also* Salsa Roja
  avocado salsa, 50
  Barbacoa, 46
  Fried Egg Tacos, 35
  Habanero Salsa, 61
  Kimchi Pico de Gallo, 60
  made to last longer, 19
  Migas, 39
  Not Spicy Restaurant-Style Salsa, 56
  Pickled Red Onions, 50
  Pineapple Salsa Verde, 55
  Salsa Borracha, 62
  Salsa de Chicharron, 65
  Salsa Roja, 52
  Salsa Verde, 50
  Salsa Verde Cruda, 57

salsa macha
  American Pizza, 186
  Chilaquiles with mole, 214
  Grilled Cheese with birria, 187
  Macha Peanut Noodles, 132
  Mexican Pizza, 186
  Pizza with mole, 215
  Pozole Rojo, 172
  Salsa Macha Marinated Goat Cheese, 66
  Sweet & Spicy Macha Wings, 192
  Watermelon Feta Salad, 123

Salsa Roja
  American Pizza, 186
  Chilaquiles, 186
  recipe, 52

sandwiches. *See also* burgers
  Chipotle Avocado BLT, 109
  Creamy Enchilada Soup with Grilled Cheese, 164
  Sloppy Jose's, 110
  Spicy Mortadella Sandwich, 107
  Sweet & Spicy Coconut Lobster (or Shrimp) Sandwich, 106
  Taki's Chicken Sandwich, 104

serrano peppers
  Chile-Lime Poke Bowls, 161
  Coconut Ceviche, 78
  Queso Panela Aguachile, 77

Ribeye Aguachile, 210
Salsa Borracha, 62
Salsa Verde, 50
Salsa Verde Cruda, 57
shrimp, in Coconut
    Ceviche, 78
Sloppy Jose's, 110
Snacking Tortillas, 24
soups
    Caldo de Albondigas,
        168
    Chicken Tortilla Soup,
        167
    Creamy Enchilada Soup
        with Grilled Cheese,
        164
    Pozole Rojo, 172
    Sopa de Fideo, 171
sour cream
    Avocado Jalapeño Dip,
        70
    Chipotle Chicken, 153
    Elote Nachos, 198
    Elote Potato Salad, 126
    Green Spaghetti, 135
    Jalapeño Popper
        Fritters, 202
    Sweet & Spicy Coconut
        Lobster (or Shrimp)
        Sandwich, 106
spaghetti
    Chori-Queso Baked
        Spaghetti, 139
    Green Spaghetti, 135
    Mexican Chicken Parm,
        157
spices, dried, 14
Spicy Mortadella
    Sandwich, 107
spinach
    Chicken Tortilla Soup,
        167
    Green Chili, 175
    Green Spaghetti, 135
    green spinach tortillas,
        23
    Mexican Lasagna, 140
    Spinach Artichoke
        Quesadillas, 144
Spinach Artichoke
    Quesadillas, 144
steak
    Bulgogi Tacos, 99
    Carne Asada, 118

Milanesa de Res, 152
Ribeye Aguachile, 210
with mole, 215
Strawberry Matcha Tres
    Leches Cake, 226
Street Corn Ravioli, 136
sweetened condensed
    milk
    Arroz con Leche y
        Mango, 225
    Chocoflan, 231
    Horchata, 221
    Pan de Elote, 229
    Strawberry Matcha Tres
        Leches Cake, 226
    Sweet & Spicy Coconut
        Lobster (or Shrimp)
        Sandwich, 106
Sweet & Spicy Coconut
    Lobster (or Shrimp)
    Sandwich, 106
Sweet & Spicy Macha
    Wings, 192

T
tacos, 84–100
    Al Pastor, 89
    Bulgogi Tacos, 99
    Carnitas, 86
    Costra de Calabaza, 95
    Fried Egg Tacos, 35
    Guac Egg Salad Tacos,
        94
    Jalapeño Popper Tacos,
        100
    Picadillo, 90
    Pork Belly Kimchi
        Tacos, 96
    Tacos de Fideo Seco, 93
Tacos de Fideo Seco, 93
Tajin
    Chile-Lime Poke Bowls,
        161
    Elote Focaccia, 201
    Elote Nachos, 198
    Elote Potato Salad, 126
    Elotes/Esquites, 197
    Pico de Gallo, 122
    Pollo Asada, 129
Taki's Chicken Sandwich,
    104
tater tots, in Tater Tot
    Breakfast Tacos, 36
Tex-Mex Enchiladas, 148
TikTok, 10, 13

tomatillos
    Chicken Tortilla Soup,
        167
    Chilaquiles Verdes, 42
    Green Chili, 175
    Mole, 212
    Pineapple Salsa Verde,
        55
    preparing, 18
    Salsa de Chicharron, 65
    Salsa Roja, 52
    Salsa Verde, 50
    Salsa Verde Cruda, 57
tomatoes. See also Roma
    tomatoes
    Cheeseburger Flautas,
        151
    Creamy Enchilada Soup
        with Grilled Cheese,
        164
    Mexican-ish Greek
        Salad, 176
    Picadillo, 90
    Sopa de Fideo, 171
    Tortas, 121
tomato sauce
    Sloppy Jose's, 110
    Tacos de Fideo Seco, 93
Tortas, 121
tortilla chips
    Cheese Stuffed Tortilla
        Chips, 73
    Chilaquiles Rojos, 43
    Chilaquiles Verdes, 42
    Chilaquiles with mole,
        214
    Elote Nachos, 198
    Green Chili with, 175
Tortilla Chips, Cheese
    Stuffed, 73
tortillas. See also Corn
    Tortillas; Flour Tortillas
    green spinach tortillas,
        23
    Snacking Tortillas, 24
    Steak with mole, 215
    for tacos, 84
tostados
    Coconut Ceviche
        served with, 78
    Queso Panela
        Aguachile served
        with, 77
tuna, in Chile-Lime Poke
    Bowls, 161

V
Valentina hot sauce, in
    Valentina Wings, 188
Valentina Wings, 188
vermicelli. See fideo
    noodles

W
waffle fries, in Chorizo
    Poutine, 209
Waffles, Honey Chipotle
    Chicken and, 205
watermelon, in
    Watermelon Feta
    Salad, 123
White Rice with Corn, 26

Z
zucchini
    Chicken Tortilla Soup,
        167
    Costra de Calabaza, 95
    Green Chili, 175

Acknowledgments

To my parents, for being my biggest cheerleaders. Literally, anyone they see, they find a way to tell them about me and how proud they are of me. Los quiero mucho. To the rest of my family, my brother, tias, tios and primos y mis amigos. Thank you for always supporting my love of food and always being there to eat all the extras, or else I'd be 600 pounds by now.

To my friends, for always keeping me humble and willing to go to back-to-back restaurants with me on trips because all that food is what keeps fueling my creativity.

To Molly & the rest of the DK & Penguin Random House team. Thank you for believing in me to write this book. I knew I always wanted to do it, but never knew how I'd make it happen. Your email changed my life & no words can explain how much I appreciate it.

To Jaime, my amazing assistant, I truly would have gone crazy and this book wouldn't of been finished if it wasn't for your keeping all my emails and calendar of deadlines on track.

Lastly, to Ivanna & Ismael, my two foodie besties and now my go to food stylist and photographer. I am sure there are days when we all wanted to strangle each other, this was the first book for all of us, it was crazy, but we freaking did it. I wouldn't have made it through this book if it wasn't for you two. We met and bonded over our love of food with zero idea what would come next. You both understood my vision for how I wanted this book to come out and you made it happen. I am forever grateful for you both coming into my life. Your work on these photos was a million times better than I ever could have imagined and I can't wait to see what you do in the future.

About the Author

Alfredo Garcia has been a full-time content creator since 2021. His love of cooking is inspired by the strong women in his family, especially his mother, grandmother, and aunts. He'd watch them as they'd make chilaquiles (easily his all time favorite meal), tacos, and every kind of salsa you can imagine. His first product, a salsa macha, is available at Freddsters.com. He resides in the Rio Grande Valley of Texas.